Populocracy

Comparative Political Economy
Series Editor: Erik Jones

A major new series exploring contemporary issues in comparative political economy. Pluralistic in approach, the books offer original, theoretically informed analyses of the interaction between politics and economics, and explore the implications for policy at the regional, national and supranational level.

Published

Europe and Northern Ireland's Future
Mary C. Murphy

The New Politics of Trade
Alasdair R. Young

Populocracy
Catherine Fieschi

Populocracy

The Tyranny of Authenticity and the Rise of Populism

Catherine Fieschi

First published in 2019 by Agenda Publishing

Agenda Publishing Limited
The Core
Bath Lane
Newcastle Helix
Newcastle upon Tyne
NE4 5TF
www.agendapub.com

ISBN 978-1-78821-024-9 (hardcover)
ISBN 978-1-78821-025-6 (paperback)

British Library Cataloguing-in-Publication Data
A catalogue record for this book is available from the British Library

Typeset by JS Typesetting Ltd, Porthcawl, Mid Glamorgan
Printed and bound in the UK by 4edge Limited

Contents

Wanting to be understood, as adults, can be, among many other things, our most violent form of nostalgia.
Adam Phillips, *Missing Out*

Acknowledgements

In writing this book I have drawn on the generosity and knowledge of a number of people who should not go unmentioned. Chief amongst them: Erik Jones as friend, editor and enthusiastic sounding board; Heather Grabbe who has been a constant and thoughtful interlocutor on these issues, and Michael Freeden whose work and insights have shaped much of the thinking behind this volume. Joel Gombin's meticulous work on the French far right and French populism has been immeasurably valuable, as has his willingness to respond to my many untimely WhatsApp queries; Finally, I have tried to heed Simon Kuper's exhortations and advice to "tell a story" as best I could.

My colleagues at Counterpoint Marley Morris, Lila Caballero-Sosa and Ulrike Grassinger, have all contributed immensely to my thinking over the past few years, and have been, crucially, wonderful companions in what can only be described at times, as unnerving research settings. Susanna Abse and David Tuckett helped me find my way through the thicket of basic psychoanalytic concepts and asked the kind of "left-field" questions that move thinking forward and shift perspective. Jamie Bartlett, Serge Bossini, Ian Bremmer, Aristos Doxiadis, Tina Fordham, John Gaffney, Eva Hoffman, Bo Lidegaard, and Sabine Selchow have all also contributed in different ways, through sustained conversations, friendly challenges, or helpful suggestions.

To all of them I am affectionately indebted. You can credit them with the best of this book, and leave all errors and major imperfections at my doorstep.

It's no secret that populism – in Europe and elsewhere – is something I have been thinking about for too long. As a former academic, in my roles in think tanks and research groups, and in various advisory capacities. It is also probably something on which I spend too much of my leisure time. So, this book is dedicated to Benjamin, Gabriele, Thomas, Jack and Nina, who I hope will spend far less of their lives thinking about populism. But that only depends on us.

Catherine Fieschi
London

Introduction

The first time I walked into Jean-Marie Le Pen's office, it was in Brussels. Having spent months trying to secure a meeting with him in Paris, I realized that it would be a lot easier to set this up at the European Parliament – where no one wanted anything to do with him.

Countless letters to the Front National's then head of press had created a tenuous connection with her: we had moved from "who are you exactly?" (a PhD student studying the FN), to "in principle, yes" ("but not now"), and finally to a relationship, of sorts, in which I donned the mantel of supplicant on a weekly basis and she magnanimously showed increasing amounts of calendar flexibility. We reached the high-point of our calendar courtship when she finally revealed the name and phone number of the woman who handled "le Chef's" appointments in Brussels and the specific dates on which I was most likely to clinch an interview.

This was summer 1996. I had a studious, academic, detailed knowledge of Jean-Marie Le Pen and his party. And I had scoured countless interviews, watched him on French television and listened to him on French radio. I had read multiple accounts of populism, in Europe and elsewhere (from the nineteenth-century Russians to the emerging Europeans, via the twentieth-century Latin Americans), examined the geography of votes, the historical lineage, the Poujade references and the links to fascism and authoritarianism. And though all of it was crucial, these strands did not manage to come together to explain the increasing amount of traction that the FN exercised over French politics, the French party system and the French, *tout-court*.

The one thing I had not done was interact with Le Pen. So, I did not know what to expect but I expected something. I expected something to fall into place that would provide me with the insight that would bring the rest together. It took years before that crucial insight finally came into focus.

At this point it is perhaps worth pointing out that what appeared obvious to me – that whatever social science framework my PhD would draw on, it would not stand up to political scrutiny unless it took into account, one way or another, the lived experiences of the person at the centre of the party, of those who worked with him, and of those who listened – this was not a view that held much sway in the corridors of North American political science. While "case studies" were deemed necessary, they were often carried out through remote data gathering, the administering of large questionnaires, and driven by rather abstract models. I did have a model, but it included quite specific humans, in quite specific contexts and circumstances.

Interviewing Le Pen, or his close entourage, as I subsequently did (and his supporters, which I also did), smacked of a kind of interpretive approach rather at odds with the variables-based, hypotheses-constructing, falsification-extracting methodology with which I am at ease, but of which I am not enamoured. Partly, because it is incomplete; and partly because it is not much fun. It is elegant, it generates beautiful models, and it creates an imperative of rigour that I continue to appreciate, indeed, respect and (hopefully) practice. But it leaves politics and the language – verbal and symbolic – of politics out. It diminishes the role of history and tends to abstract from context. I am hoping that this text brings both of these approaches together: the elegance of the comparative method and the rich fun of political experience.

Bonjour Monsieur Le Pen

Walking into one of the clinical booths that pass for offices in the European Parliament, I was struck by how easy this was. I cannot quite emphasize enough the contrast between the professional, frictionless access I was granted in that moment and the sulphurous coverage that surrounded the man I was about to meet. The latter all the more present in my mind given that this was the culmination of months of planning and, frankly, just making a nuisance of myself.

Yet on this very bright day, there he was, in a three-piece suit sitting behind a bare desk whose pristine order said much about the nature of his presence at the European Parliament. This did not appear to be a place of work: it was a question of being there, marking time and presence rather than doing much else. This was also a time when the FN shared their office with the Belgian far right party, Vlaams Blok (now Vlaams Belang). The area they all occupied felt a little like the "naughty corner": it was out of the way, down even more – and even more deserted – corridors than other party offices. And it felt quiet and empty: a couple of FN posters on the wall, a handful of FN MEPs looking suitably louche in this temple of technocracy and democracy, and a few marooned Vlaams Blok MEPs in bad suits, were all that was visible.

Walking into the office and shaking his hand provided a curious contrast: the hulking presence and booming voice filled the room; and yet there was nothing particularly striking about the man: he looked average. He could easily have been one of the guys hollering and heckling behind a market-stall.

As we sat down, and *he* asked question upon question (to which *he* replied), his manner became almost manic. It was extremely difficult to get a word in edgewise. Over the course of the next few hours, this mountain of a man (known to his friends and colleagues as "*le menhir*" – the standing stone – a reference to his native Brittany, but also to his sheer size and presence) would sing, dance, laugh, flirt. And lie.

Tell me lies

Everything I thought I knew about him – from his date of birth, to the accident that led to his having long worn an eye-patch, to the circumstances of his father's death, to who his friends were, as well as who his enemies could be – was called into question. Even within one conversation Le Pen managed to trip himself up – getting the dates wrong, or events he'd just related in the wrong order. It felt like a poor amateur detective play: did I say with the dagger in the library? I meant with the candlestick in the study. People referred to as friends in one breath, were summarily dismissed as traitors in the next.

Part of the discomfort was the contrast between physical heft and immovable solidity – and an approach to narrative that was the very opposite: uncontrolled, manic, almost demented. Over time, I realized that this was, in fact, an incredibly effective control mechanism: it scrambled the wires and kept you permanently off balance, confused and guessing. What exactly was one meant to hear, or make of the stories? How much was he inventing, and how much was one – was I – misremembering?

It was impossible to take notes, so over the next few years, I took to recording him. But sometimes, I didn't; I'd pretend I'd forgotten my recorder, to see if it made any difference to style and content. It did not. And it dawned on me over time, that the audience did not really matter much either; that what mattered were two things. First, the stage from which he imagined he was speaking. Political stages are a bit like real stages: metaphorically speaking, when you're on one, and the house-lights are off, you cannot see your audience, and you'd probably rather not. But what matters to the actor is the imagined audience. Le Pen knew exactly the France he was speaking to and the history they shared. He did not need to see them – or me. And he certainly did not feel he was in a dialogue with them. It was pure broadcast.

The second important point had to do with the lying, with the stories he was spinning, with the blatant untruths he chose to speak, and the shamelessness with which he did so. It took me a while to realize that what Le Pen was spinning in these intimate settings were political tests of civility. Would I point out the lie? The courage was not only his to be had for lying so obviously, it was a test of my own courage (as a "young left-wing woman" as he once characterized me!) and capacity to get over a sort of bourgeois embarrassment that would prevent me from saying, hang on, that doesn't make any sense, that's not what you said last time. And the lying was not of the sort that one might hope to cover-up. He was not lying with the aim of not getting caught out. Quite the opposite: the evidence of a lie was the point. Especially if it flew in the face of public knowledge. And this went right to the heart of the matter: that while I was shocked at this obvious transgression of a democratic norm of truth-telling, he was displaying a complete disregard for it. And this transgression was the basis of his whole politics.

But while Jean-Marie Le Pen easily lied one-on-one, he seldom did so on a grand scale: he took care not to spin grand untruths and total lies on prime television for example. On those occasions, he never entirely made the jump from an inference to an assertion. Not in his nasty holocaust denial, nor even more simply in the use of crime or immigration statistics. These were used to infer, to lead-on, but by and large, there were no assertions of blatant untruths. No fabrication of lies in the national limelight – although he made plenty of accusations of fabrications by others. The lies which he instinctively told, his manner of recounting a story in ways in which fact, half-fact and fiction collided, would become the modus operandi of a whole generation of populist politicians. Over time, his successors in liberal democracies would grow to develop a fine line in this sort of behaviour, in contexts and with citizens who would be increasingly ready to forgive them and even to reward them for it.

1

What is it about populism?

Three main reasons prompted me to write this book. The first two fall, by and large, into the category of "explanation" or "clarification". When I first started to become interested in populism, it was a minority sport. I was interested in Thatcherism and wrote an MA thesis about her politics and its place within the British political tradition. I discovered the writings of Stuart Hall on authoritarian populism, and, as a 20 year-old, became enraptured with his forensic capacity to expose the ideological springs of a truly novel political experiment. Hall's debates with Bob Jessop in the *New Left Review* were my first, real foray into political analysis that took ideology seriously. It led me to take it so seriously that I became interested in "the stronger stuff". Thatcher was riveting, but I concluded that, in terms of populism, she was not the Real McCoy. Her resignation coincided with my typing up of the final version of my MA – I typed as quickly as I could as events came to a head, keeping just enough of an eye on the television to make sure she was not doing or saying anything that would blow my little thesis apart. Pre-social media, pre-internet, I could not leave the house for fear of missing someone being pushed down the stairs in Downing Street. As I write in March 2019, it's funny how history repeats itself, except now I can find out more easily who are the latest casualties, or survivors.

Thatcher was also resigning just as the French Front National (FN) was emerging as a powerful political force, and Europe started to take notice. So, I turned my attention to it and to Jean-Marie Le Pen – the early bubblings of European populism. I was asked relatively often at the time, why I had chosen such a "niche" topic for my PhD. Then, a dissertation on populism was considered highly original, bordering on the quirky. Now, when I reveal my special subject, I am almost met with a yawn. Surely not another populism specialist? So, the first question I want to answer in this volume is why (brushing aside the possibility that

I was staggeringly prescient) populism has become such a common-place feature of our politics. What has happened in the last thirty years to account for the exponential success of populist parties, and for the impact of populist politics on our political landscapes?

The second reason that prompted me to write this book is to do with the number of times I am confronted with interlocutors who seem to be waiting for – in fact expecting – things to "go back to normal" as they put it, "once the effects of the financial crisis are over", "once the econ-omy picks up", or "we create more jobs", "we curb immigration", or "we protect fragile industries". Surely, the roller coaster will stop? One of the key aims of this book is to show that, while there is no reason why we may not return to a less polarized or fragmented politics at some point (just as we may not), the important point is that the political and insti-tutional settlement on which we do so, will probably be fundamentally different – this, as the cliché goes, is the new normal. So, part of my aim is to show what political boundaries we have crossed over recent years and how populist politics – a political outlook that has encouraged deep polarization, challenged the status quo that we took for granted, and allowed new actors to burst onto the scene – has achieved this.

Who can we blame for the nature of current politics? The financial and economic dislocation unleashed by financial capitalism and culmi-nating in the effects of the 2008 economic crash? Was it the paradoxical result of both economic and social progress and political parties failing to adapt to new voter expectations? Did our relationship, as citizens, to "the political class" change fundamentally, and if so, how and why? Was it simply growing inequality, despite rising levels of wealth? Or, was it the experience of cultural and social changes that led some citizens to feel that they were being routinely excluded from the collective cultural norms of their homeland? And do any of these explanations account for the spectacle of mature democracies struggling to manage political debate and policy-making under the weight of growing polarization and conflict?

And so, to my third, and most important, reason which is about ask-ing the right questions. The fact is that we do have some idea of what has caused populist politics to take hold. The work produced by scholars, think tanks, pollsters and journalists in this area is good. It is search-ing and thorough as the next section shows. Therefore, we know very well that populist politics are the result of all of the things listed above colliding into each other and conspiring to create the kind of tectonic economic and social change that is bound to affect politics fundamentally – because it is bound to stretch the capacities of existing institutions, and, in the end, people's trust in them.

As we look to the causes and drivers of populism, we can come to realize that we are pretty good now at pointing to some of the key dynamics that account for why voters choose it. For example, we know that economic deprivation plays a role. Which means that we also know that inequality and the perception of inequality will fuel resentment against those who are seen to benefit, or who fail to suffer "equally", from such hardships. We know that, in places such as the UK, the austerity that followed the financial crisis will have exacerbated a sense of personal and collective vulnerability but also of national decline, and that this will have had consequences for perceptions of Europe and its role. And we know that the experience of stretched welfare systems and the lack of a sense of protection will have reinforced the impression (and the traumatic realization) that the institutions of the state were no longer able, or willing, to protect or cushion from economic blows. And we know that this caused a backlash against those governments and mainstream politicians who were seen as complicit. Whether this is a failure to protect from austerity measures, or a failure to cushion against major transformations in the labour market, makes little difference (Wagner 2014). Just as those who were seen as complicit in the creation of a culture that excluded aspects of more traditional outlooks and values, also carried the blame for creating a sense of exclusion; for giving other members of their society the impression that they were "second-class citizens". And finally, we know that social, economic and technological transformations have refashioned people's preferences, and therefore led them to abandon parties, join others, or simply completely re-evaluate or, even give up on, the norms and values of mainstream politics. Taken together, this is a pretty comprehensive understanding of the springs of support for populist parties in western societies. And there are a number of excellent accounts of such developments, and how they work together and reinforce each other (see Eatwell & Goodwin 2018; Temin 2017; Hoschild 2016).

We are even perfectly capable of understanding that, in their deep entwining, such causes mean that job growth, curbing immigration, or more money for public services each on its own will not make populist politics go away. And we can even acknowledge that part of the issue is that results take a long time, that our economies and societies are undergoing transformative shifts that they will have to ride out over years, that people are, rightly, impatient and that governments over-promise.

And yet we remain puzzled. Because, in part, such politics seldom deliver much to their supporters; but mainly because these dynamics do not really account for the quality – the type, texture and feel – of the politics to which populism gives rise.

The first part of the puzzle is about the form of politics: although we understand the source of the resentment, we do not understand why it should be expressed, in so many places, in this particular, populist, form. This makes us suspect, quite rightly, that there is something else driving politics in this direction. And not only that, but that the general direction of travel is redefining democratic politics, not necessarily away from democracy, but certainly away from the democracy we have come to know. That we have passed a point of no return, so that whatever comes next will look different.

The second part of the puzzle has to do with the quality of the politics: there is something about the nature of the resentment that does not seem to connect to its expression. Not because the behaviour is unlikely to deliver to the voter base[1], but because there seems to be a mismatch between the crass, superficial, often destructive nature of populist politics and the understandable, well-founded resentments and longings that fuel it. The problem is that this may lead us to ask the wrong questions, such as why people believe in lies or fake news (and how can we change their minds), when what we should be asking is what role these play in the new political landscape. Or we puzzle over declining levels of trust in some institutions, when perhaps trust is no longer the "political currency" we should be focusing on.

What this book seeks to do is to tilt the lens toward that gap between the resentment and the quality of our politics in western democracies at the moment and to see what ideas and motivations live there. And also to give pride of place to the way in which a certain set of transformations have come together to create a wildly hospitable culture (including hospitable citizens) for populist ideas and populist politics. First by looking at some of the best accounts. And then by suggesting what else should

---

1. This is a question wonderfully explored – and answered – in Frank 2004.

be factored in to help us make sense of the political culture we have created, and move, at the very least, from puzzlement to realisation – to foresight.

Populism?

Populism has dictated the tempo of politics in western democracies: it has imposed an agenda, challenged mainstream parties and is shaping policy. It has set in motion Brexit, constrained Angela Merkel, reshaped Italy's relationship to Europe, reshaped Europe's relationship to Russia and, via Donald Trump, called into question 50 years of Pax Americana. But what is it exactly?

The paradox is that, as populism has become more and more of a recognized political force in its own right, its boundaries have become hazier. Once no more than an exotic sideshow – either redolent of failed democratic development or treated as a hangover from fascism – populism has become the political weather. Lately, diagnoses – or rather accusations – of populism have rung out as soon as any political leader has called for the mobilization of their constituency. Any *popular* measure is promptly labelled *populist*. Just as any measure that serves the interests of "most people" is often similarly mis-labelled populist: recall, UK readers, the accusations levelled at Ed Miliband when, as leader of the opposition Labour Party, he suggested holding private energy companies accountable. What might have hitherto been taken as no more than a relatively classic social democratic proposal, was immediately branded "populist demagoguery".

Our difficulty in defining this sort of politics, means that it was long relegated to the "second division" of politics. Populism just did not have the heft and gravitas of fascism, socialism or liberalism. And so, studies of populism often downgraded their own subject matter to the status of an "ingredient" in the bigger, more serious ideological forms: populism was part of fascism, or an aspect of Conservatism; but it could not stand on its own, as it were, to mobilize voters, because it was thought to lack a defined political project. Some authors referred to it as a "thin centred" ideology; others referred to the "empty heart" of populism (Taggart 2004). Two expressions that suggest superficiality: populism was seen as all style and no substance. Indeed, many scholars initially focused on populism as no more than a form of leadership. Populist politics were inextricably tied to, even equated with, rhetoric that goes hand in hand with an almost pantomime charismatic leader (with little clarity on what that elusive charismatic quality was): it was fascism without the teeth. Populism was Juan Peron on a balcony, Pierre Poujade and his petty bourgeois charisma, the rousing tones of a Jean-Marie Le Pen haranguing his supporters for hours on end, or, more recently, Nigel Farage lambasting his fellow MEPs in the European Parliament. Those perspectives hindered the understanding of populism as a definable political doctrine that can give rise, potentially, to political programmes with bona fide followers and voters.

With populist parties now centre-stage across western democracies, with voters rallying to its appeals and flocking to its political proposals (however simplistic), and with certain leaders such as France's Jean Luc Mélenchon ("Me, a populist? And proud of it too"[2]), Spain's Pablo Iglesias, or Italy's Beppe Grillo[3] adopting the label with a certain relish despite its often-stigmatizing effect, the status and role of populism need to be re-examined and the nature and source of its power are worth revisiting. I am not suggesting, by the way, that the populist transformation is as new as the attention it has received (certainly this has been a long time coming, flickers appearing as far back as the mid-1950s in Europe), but it is new in the sense that it is postwar; in many ways, it is the first tectonic democratic transformation to take place since the great push for representative democracy in the earlier part of the twentieth century that saw the various waves of demand for suffrage extension and workers' representation. Part of the difficulty is that, to paraphrase Potter Stewart, we know populism when we see it, but its observers are often thwarted by its variety. Attempts to move beyond surface resemblances can often feel like one long list of caveats.

Across Europe and the United States a host of parties and personalities have triggered the not-so-exclusive appellation: Italy's M5S and also the Lega, Law and Justice in Poland, Marine Le Pen (and of course

2. Jean-Luc Mélenchon, interview in *L'Express*, 16 September 2010.
3. "M5S is neither left nor right [...] it is *proudly populist*", Beppe Grillo blog, 14 December 2013 (emphasis in the original): http://www.beppegrillo.it/il-m5s-e-populista-ne-di-destra-ne-di-sinistra-fieramentepopulista/ (accessed 15 March 2019).

her father), but also Jean-Luc Mélenchon in France, Germany's AfD, Spain's Podemos, the American Republican party under Trump, the PVV in the Netherlands, UKIP in the UK, the Austrian FPÖ of course, but also the Austrian OVP under its current leader Sebastian Kurz. In some cases, the populist quality of these parties and movements seems irredeemably tied to their leaders (see Wilders and the PVV, UKIP and Nigel Farage) and in others less so (Italy's Lega was a populist party long before Salvini, for instance, and the Republican party, as do all the other parties of which he was a member, exists without Trump – at least one hopes). We shall examine the relationship to leadership later on. The point here is that these parties are sometimes on the left and sometimes on the right; that some are nativist, and some are not; that some are anti-immigration and some are not; some are pro-welfare and others less so. And as they become fixtures in the political landscape, their stances change, and their electorates evolve, as would those of any party. But whereas most parties and movements might have a solid body of writing or political tradition to anchor their stances, populism does not.

The one kernel of agreement across scholars, analysts and observers is that the line of division between the people and an undeserving elite is the fundamental one around which populist politics is organized. In very basic terms, the people/elite divide plays much the same role as the capital/workers divide might have played in socialist politics. But this doesn't tell us much about the antagonisms between these two protagonists, their respective roles in the developments that led to populist party evolution, or the sources of resentment, the proposed solutions (whether plausible or implausible), the relationship to institutions, or what might make this line of division more salient at some points, and in some contexts, than in others. The title of this book aims to highlight that whatever the mechanisms at play, the spread of populist politics reflects the growing ease and success with which the people/elite divide is routinely used to mobilize voters and, more broadly citizens.

Mirroring the spread of populist politics, the study of populism has become a growth industry – one eminent editor of a scholarly journal told me it could easily have become the *Journal of Populist Studies* given the number of submissions on the topic. So just for the sake of clarity, below is a broad outline of what most analysts have privileged when they examine populism. Aside from clearing a space for thought, the various approaches give us a strong sense of the various ways in which populism has been conceptualized as a political phenomenon and where we might need to add to this.

Defining populism by explaining how we got here

There are almost as many ways of slicing the populist cake as there are populism scholars – and there are legions of the latter. For our purposes here, what interests us are the main drivers of populism's emergence as seen by some of its key analysts. What they include, but also of course what they leave out.

Democracy's broken promises: populism as a symptom of disillusionment

A number of approaches could fall under the heading "the pitfalls of representative democracy". All of the analysts in this camp (including myself as an occasional member; Fieschi 2013) have posited a deep link between tensions that are inherent in democratic institutions and the rise of populism. For most of these analysts, populism is an almost inevitable symptom (more or less welcome depending on the scholar) of democracy's fundamental contradictions, many of which have appeared under the pressure of capitalism's transformations, inadequately updated institutions, a changing media and unfulfilled redistributive promises.

For Cas Mudde and Cristobal Rovira Kaltwasser, for example, populism could potentially be a "corrective to democracy": what the authors refer to as an "illiberal democratic response to undemocratic liberalism" (Mudde & Kaltwasser 2013). In a nutshell: when democracy stops being true to its promises, voters and citizens more broadly, will call it out, even if that means resorting to illiberal means or programmes. Indeed, for some, populism can veer into "democratic extremism", the temptation to resort to democracy's least appealing and most potentially exclusive or oppressive features, in order to protect its promises. Populist figures such as Marine Le Pen, or Geert Wilders are not above rejecting Islam in the name of the values of liberal democracy, regardless of the injury to liberal democracy itself.

In a related vein, scholars such as Margaret Canovan spoke of populism as a "shadow cast by democracy" (Canovan 1981). This was an important contribution because it was one of the very first acknowledgements that democracy was not the opposite of populism, but rather intricately linked to it. In many respects, populism is dependent on democracy, and democracy itself contains the seeds of populism. In a 1999 article, Canovan went further: populism was more than a shadow cast by democracy, it was in fact the inevitable result of the interaction of what she called the "two faces of democracy" (Canovan 1999; Arditi 2004). Democracy, she argued, is a permanent tussle between its heroic face – "the promise of a better world through the action of a sovereign people" (Canovan 1999: 12) – and its pragmatic one, which she refers to as the "grubby business of politics", all the practices and mechanisms that are so many ways of dealing with conflict without resorting to repression or violence. Populism, she concludes, occurs when the gap between these two aspects of democracy appears too great and pragmatism seems to overtake the heroic dimension of politics. In the face of too much dealing and manoeuvring (or technocratic managing), populism emerges in an attempt to fill the widening gap and reassert the people's need to re-establish control over some key areas of their lives (*ibid.*).

Some analysts argue that paying too much attention to the relationship between democracy and populism is unhelpful (see Stavrakakis & Jager 2018). But events over the past few decades illustrate that this relationship is foundational, that there is no populism without democracy, and that populism arises, in great part, from a perception of betrayal of the democratic promise and the high-jacking of the dividends of democracy by an elite. You could even argue that the greater the foundational promise of equality, the greater the chances of populist politics emerging once this promise is perceived as broken (whether because a new elite has emerged – the media, the bureaucracy, civil servants, banks – or because leaders are seen as corrupt, or because they are seen as having developed separate interests from those of the people they claim to work for). The United States, France, Germany, and developments in the more successfully "transitioned" central and eastern European countries (Poland, Hungary) tend to bear out this paradox: the greater and more explicit the democratic promise, the more painful its potential let-downs, the greater the likelihood of populist politics. Interestingly, this sort of explanation is not a million miles from E. P. Thompson's analysis of eighteenth-century bread riots in the English countryside. In Thompson's explanation the rebellions took place because an unspoken contract – a convention – around the fair price of bread and other essential goods was replaced by free market principles (Thompson 1971). In the case of populism, the people demand that the – far more explicit – democratic contract be honoured. In both cases, there is a relative conservatism at play, despite the chaotic and sometimes revolutionary slogans of the movements, a desire to return to a safer, fairer past is usually detectable.

The result of economic dislocation?

In discussions on populism the roles of deprivation (whether absolute or relative), inequality and economic dislocation often take centre stage. For a number of observers and analysts, there is no escaping the fact that populism has dramatically progressed in Europe and in the United States since the recession of 2008 and the euro crisis that followed. Aside from the fact that this view tends to suffer from relative amnesia (parties such as the French FN or the Dutch PVV took off long before 2008) there is a broader argument about the impact of a particular version of capitalism that cannot be dismissed so easily.

Here the argument is that it is not necessarily capitalism per se but the growing spread of its neoliberal version from the 1980s onwards (one that encourages state retrenchment and a severely redesigned, more conditional welfare state) that is to blame for the rise of populism in western democracies. Thatcherism and Reaganism are often taken as the starting point of what many see as the unravelling of the post-war economic consensus. For someone like David Harvey (2007) the premises of this neoliberalism are that "human well-being can best be advanced by liberating individual entrepreneurial freedoms and skills within an institutional framework characterized by strong private property rights, free markets and free trade. The role of the state is to create and preserve an institutional framework appropriate to such practices" (Harvey 2010: 2). Economic deregulation, the selling of state assets (think of Thatcher's privatization of housing and of the North Sea oil reserves) and the shrinking role of the state to increase flexibility and avoid any bureaucratic or ideological hindrances complete the package.

Add to this more recent developments around the transformation of work – automation and artificial intelligence – and it is no wonder that citizens might feel that the system that seems to benefit an international elite (comprised of bankers and multinationals, but also of the politicians who enable them) has sold them out. The state no longer protects them. The fact that this very same elite bent over backwards to use public funds to bail-out banks in 2008 was the insult to the injury that might have helped to unleash the public backlash.

In a 2014 paper, Markus Wagner explores the various emotions triggered by the financial crisis in Britain. The paper is particularly enlightening because it illustrates pointedly the link between blame and anger. Wagner makes a set of interesting points related to the difference between anger and fear (Wagner 2014: 685). His research tends to show that if people can blame someone, then they will tend to get angry, whereas if they are unable to apportion blame, they will tend to be fearful. In other words, Wagner argues, fear is the default position, anger only develops when people can blame someone; they get angrier still if that person or institution is seen as having broken a promise; and more to the point for the argument that follows here, they tend to get angry if they feel they should be able to control the actor inflicting this on them, when they, themselves should be able to affect the situation. But as pointed out by Wagner, "The question is not whether individuals have actual control over the external actor, but whether they believe they should have such control. In sum, angry emotional reactions may arise in particular when voters blame an actor with whom the principal-agent relationship is malfunctioning" (*ibid.*: 689), or put another way – when someone appointed to act on your behalf is no longer seen to be doing so.

This is where the argument becomes most interesting. The fact is that economic hardship or inequality alone do not seem to trigger angry reactions. As pointed out by Guido Alfani:

> The new data now available [...] suggest that in the last seven centuries of European history, the general tendency has been for inequality to increase [...] The only two phases of significant decline in inequality which occurred in the last seven centuries [...] were triggered by some of the largest shocks recorded in human history: the Black Death in the fourteenth century and the two world wars in the twentieth. (Alfani 2018: 13–17)

But as Alfani goes on to argue, this was mediated by institutions and institutional change: the "lull" in inequality after the end of the Second World War was the result of progressive taxation and the redistributive policies of the welfare state from the end of the war to the end of the 1970s. So, the point is not only that institutions are key to mediating these experiences and the emotions to which they give rise, but also that it takes more than economic hardship or a perception of deprivation alone to give rise to these emotions – injustice and blame need to come into it. And at that point it is very difficult to separate out the effect of economic shock from how these are institutionally and culturally mediated.

Cultural backlash?

So, another strand of analysis, in fact, explains populism as just that: a cultural backlash. Here populism is depicted as the protest of those who feel culturally left behind and want to "stick it" to the elite and its political representatives. Long before this became a public debate, political science zeroed in on what Ronald Inglehart summarized as a shift away from materialist values that were foundational to the left/right divide (values that revolved around redistribution, social protection and the role of the state vis-à-vis the market) to what he called "post-materialist" values (anchored around topics such as authority, sexual freedoms, or diversity). The cultural backlash explanation is in part designed to address the growth of working-class support for populist stances. Here the conversion of many social democratic parties away from "bread and butter" issues to these post-materialist "politics of recognition" (embodied by multicultural policies, anti-discrimination legislation, promotion of gender equality to name a few) is seen as an explanation for the growth of a populist backlash as voters felt abandoned by their traditional champions (Inglehart & Norris 2018; Eribon 2009).

A number of writers and analysts have made the point that the prioritization of immigration over the protection of borders has given rise to various forms of cultural insecurities, and a sense of marginalization (Goodhart 2017; Bouvet 2015). Both of which feed into the readiness of working-class voters to embrace options more traditionally associated with the right. The resentment creates a wave of nostalgia for an imagined, "diversity-free" past that is thought to be better than the present because it seemed better at protecting the interests of national populations. While such analyses sometimes include references to the resurgence of class politics, they tend to fall more squarely into the cultural backlash assumption, including a backlash against what they feel is the self-righteousness of a liberal elite disconnected from, and unwilling to take seriously, those that Hillary Clinton refers to as "the deplorables" (Bouvet 2015 and Vance 2016 are emblematic of this position). In other words, while some may claim that this is about an exclusionary capitalist system, the backlash analysts privilege cultural relegation (or at best, relative deprivation) as the major explanation behind the rise of populism (Eatwell & Goodwin 2018).

Too much energy has been spent pitting economically-driven explanations against cultural ones, when in fact the two are deeply intertwined. As Martin Sandbu synthesizes deftly:

> The big economic changes that have transformed Western societies during the past three to four decades have worked against one particular group of the population: they have worked against the low-skilled, against the uncredentialled, and those lacking social connections to economic gatekeepers (i.e. the elite), against those loyal or tied to places in decline, against those less comfortable with changing themselves or the change in the world around them, and finally against individuals with more traditional conceptions of men's and women's work (Sandbu 2018: 35).

These attributes define particular communities (even if these are not always geographically defined) – they are, in social science jargon, "reinforcing cleavages" – they do not cut across groups but rather, tend to define one group because the cultural and economic indicators reinforce each other. They point to communities that are united in expectations (they did well after the Second World War), and united in their disappointments (they lost out the most from the changes of the past four decades). And are therefore now increasingly united in their political, social and cultural demands.

It is time to reconcile the cultural and economic explanations – each only makes sense in the context of the other. Privileging one explanation over the other leads to unrealistic expectations: that full employment will be enough to make people feel valued, or that curtailing immigration will be enough to restore their sense of belonging. Neither of them ever works on its own. And while governments address one, populist parties instrumentalize the other. It is clear that taking these grievances seriously begins by an understanding of the way they are inextricably entwined. And how populist parties and politicians are able to toggle between the two.

Populism as the expression of crisis

Cutting across a lot of the discussion on populism is the recurring theme of crisis. Whatever else may be at play, most analysts see populism as the symptom of a crisis: a crisis of democracy, a crisis of representation, an economic crisis, or more broadly a crisis of the status quo. But for some social theorists, crisis is at the root of their approach itself. As Ernesto Laclau – one of social theory's best-known scholars of populism – writes, "a crisis of representation is always at the root of any populist, anti-institutional outburst" (Laclau 2005: 139). So, similarly, for Yannis Stavrakakis, "the emergence of new discourses and new identities is always related to the *dislocation* or crisis of previously hegemonic discursive orders … this is also the case with populist discourses" (Stavrakakis 2000: 247). For these scholars, populism is "the structuring logic of political life", since all politics is articulated against a reigning consensus (Howarth, Norval & Stavrakakis 2000). Such an approach is of limited applicability for those of us interested in comparative analysis, but the notion of populism as a "logic" rather than as a "thing" is useful. That logic according to Panizza "simplifies the political space by symbolically dividing society between 'the people' (as the 'underdogs') and its 'other'" (Panizza 2005: 3). This work reminds us that populism, like any other political phenomenon is highly symbolic. In fact, it can be argued that its power is derived as much from its symbolic content as from the actual, real events that take place. For instance, the election of Donald Trump is an undeniable reality, but the way in which his presidency works is as much, if not more, about the manner in which he performs his presidency as responding to a set of crises (the "carnage" that is taking place in American cities, or the "humanitarian crisis" he evokes at the US–Mexico border for instance) in social media, the way it is discussed by the media and other pundits, as it is about the policies he enacts – which are of course always part-symbol.

But the work on the relationship between crisis and populism also reminds us that populism does not just emerge as a result of a crisis, but that its logic is also to *create* crisis. Benjamin Moffitt makes an important point when he argues that populist politics also seek to trigger crisis (Moffitt 2015). Here the triggering of crisis is described as a process that goes from identifying failure, to turning this failure into a crisis[4] by linking it to a particular identity (that is framed as under threat), identifying those who can be blamed for this failure, using the media to propagate the message and then putting forward a simplistic solution rooted in strong leadership to resolve the crisis. And repeat (*ibid.*: 198). This cycle is easy to identify and Matteo Salvini's attitude toward migrant ships in the summer of 2018 is an excellent illustration of this script at work: point to a failure of the EU migration framework, frame it as the EU using Italy as its cheap migrant repository (as opposed to valued partner), tweet and use Facebook liberally to grow the impression of crisis (whilst in fact crossings across the Mediterranean were at a record low) and prevent ships from docking in Italy as the solution.

Beyond the exploitation and triggering of crisis, the broader question of populism as disruptive politics strikes us as crucial in the relationship it develops with voters. The approaches outlined here, as influential as they are, tend to depict populism as something that arises a little like a "Deus ex machina", as though a set of circumstances (late capitalism, neoliberalism, globalization) were enough to bring populism into existence. It is not that ideas do not matter to these authors, but rather that what matters most are *their* ideas about populism, rather than what populist voters and movements might latch on to. Populism goes back to being – or remains – "all dynamics" and no core. In practice, and in reality, circumstances lead to the development of a particular set of ideas that in turn acquire a certain currency and then potency by becoming the traditional backbone of populist political appeals.

In the next chapter I want to look at which ideas matter and why; and how they relate to one another to form a particular populist logic.

---

4. A useful discussion of the distinction between "failure" and "crisis" can be found in Hay 1995.

This is the only way to answer the key question which is, why the circumstances outlined in this chapter should lead to populist politics rather than another form of radical politics? After all, whether this is about crisis, about economics, or about a cultural backlash, the political reaction could have been funnelled into a different politics of contestation. Circumstances could have fuelled radical Green politics (some of which we might be beginning to see), revived socialism rather than killed it (*pace* Jeremy Corbyn's moment), led to increased demands for increased powers to international institutions, or the very opposite, demands for radical hyper-local democracy. Instead, all these alternatives have remained embryonic so far, and politics has taken the form of a politics that reaffirms old forms of sovereignty, welfare chauvinism, the supremacy of the nation-state and the reaffirmation of borders. Why? First, we need to look at ideas and then at citizens.

2

The ideas that matter, or populism as jiu-jitsu politics

One way of understanding how we find ourselves in this political moment is to understand better the ideas that make up populism. What is it that populist politicians say, believe, claim to believe, value, promise, that seems so convincing in the context we are in? At a time when political choices can seem increasingly volatile and polarized, a deeper understanding of which "packages of ideas" move people to action is crucial. And ideologies are just that: the link between ideas and mobilization of any type, whether casting a ballot, taking to the streets, staging a rally, writing a manifesto, or creating a hashtag.

Looking at the ideas that make up populism, and how these hang together as an ideology, can serve as a lens through which to track populism over time: if we can identify these key ideas and how these become more or less prominent – in relation to how they are being used and defined by political parties, movements and leaders – then we can start to tell populism from everything else because we will have a better idea of its boundaries. We can also track how it has evolved in different places and over time, and from what kind of "oxygen" it has benefited to become defining of our political era. But, equally importantly, we can track some of our own transformations as citizens and explain why we have become so susceptible to it.

Why thinking about ideologies helps

There are some clear advantages to treating populism as an ideology, as a set of ideas and the ideals that hang together as a blueprint for political action. The main advantage is that it forces observers to see it as more than a sum of its parts; it gives it some coherence and direction. In a word, it allows us to deal with populism as a political project (outlined by some and acquiesced to by others) rather than just "a development" or a symptom.

Because they help mobilize people, ideologies are more than just political thought: they contain a recommended, normative course of action. In this respect, as pointed out by political theorist Michael Freeden, ideologies are in a constant struggle with each other to establish a consensus over how the ideas they hold particularly dear should be understood (Freeden 1998: 77). It is that struggle that accounts for polarization. For example, proponents of liberalism want to establish a general consensus (through rhetoric and policy) on the fact that, in an ideal world, freedom should matter more than, say, authority. A socialist, on the other hand, might want to establish that equality should matter more than freedom. This is important: it means that ideologies in their struggle to dominate public and political life are ways of agreeing what the consensus is, or, sometimes, ways of trying to create a new consensus. Think of it as a tug of war of ideas and words, with different sides fighting over some crucial ground and attempting to pull others into it. Populist politics in the western world since the 1980s can be in part understood as a sustained attempt to "create" a new consensus (often under the guise of "revealing" the "real" – in this case the silent majority's – consensus) to replace the postwar liberal consensus. The new populist consensus might for instance insist that decision-making should be based on pure majorities rather than on respecting the rights of minorities. In this respect, populism is an ideological project: it is an attempt to create a form of consensus around a set of ideas, and therefore impose the views and the policies that might help secure it. I want to show that populism has developed a core of ideas that hang together according to a particular logic, which shapes both a world view, and the parameters of action. And that that logic has become increasingly compelling as it resonates with changing citizen preferences and expectations.

The core of an ideology can be made up of different concepts, but they are all essential. If one goes missing the ideology changes fundamentally. For example, in the case of liberalism, if freedom were to disappear, we would probably no longer really be dealing with liberalism. If a reverence for the past and history were to no longer be a core part of the Conservative Party manifesto, then it would start to feel as though it were no longer Conservatism. Similarly, for populism it would be impossible to define it without starting from its own self-reference to the idea of "the people". More on this in a moment.

These key ideas are placed into context and given colour and a richer meaning by secondary ideas and concepts. These are ideas and concepts that are important but not essential. They do a lot of the heavy contextual lifting, and they help to link core ideas together, and, ultimately, allow us to interpret the core ideas in ways that make sense at a given historical moment, in a specific place. So, they are important too.

But once we can agree that ideas matter, the next question is which ideas can we pinpoint as constants across these movements and parties in order to track their evolution? And also, which movements and parties to exclude? Not in some fit of taxonomic zeal, but because our understanding of populism (and responding to the grievances to which some of its supporters give voice) depends on being able to identify populism with some confidence, or at least with less confusion. In the next section I want to isolate the key ideas that make populism powerful, and show how they relate to each other.

Populism's not-so-empty heart

The people

One thing that all observers and scholars of populism seem to agree on is that populism rests on a conception of society in which the divide between the people and the elites is the main faultline around which conflict emerges and power is organized. Cas Mudde's widely referenced definition of populism refers to it as "a thin centred" ideology that considers society to be ultimately separated into two homogeneous and antagonistic groups, "the pure people" and "the corrupt elite", and which argues that politics should be an expression of the "*volonté générale* (general will) of the people" (Mudde 2007: 23). And I myself, have used similar language (Fieschi 2004a, 2013). Society is defined by the battle that the people wage against a corrupt elite that has usurped its power. Furthermore, populist politicians accuse this elite of claiming to have ordinary people's concerns at heart, when in fact it is solely motivated by its own distinct interests. A good illustration of this – both across Europe and in the United States – is the accusation that the elite is in favour of more immigration because it keeps wages down (this goes for the financial elite) and conforms to a cosmopolitan ideal that ordinary people do not share (this goes for the progressive or left elite). More specifically, recall the many accusations made against the European Union by the Italian Lega or the French RN (to name but two) as *ostensibly* an instrument of democratic governance and peace-keeping for all European peoples, when *in reality*, they argue, it is nothing but an elite project designed to keep wages low and goods and people flowing across borders for the benefit of business.

The role of this fundamental division between the people and the elite (or the establishment) in populist politics deserves some attention because its importance is often misunderstood. It is crucial to point out that the elite in question is not necessarily a capitalist, economic elite (it can be, and it often is, but it does not have to be – and most often it is that, as well as other things). This distinction matters because if the divide were only economic, there would be little, or no, distinction between populism and socialism. A quick look at a Donald Trump suggests that the resentment in the US is not only, or even mainly, against the rich, but against the connected, the metropolitans, the liberals (who are often branded hypocrites). The same can be said about the UK Independence Party (UKIP) supporters, or the radically left-wing populist France Insoumise (FI) supporters in France; the super-rich may get it in the neck, but the super-connected, or the super-liberal even more so.

What is being fought over are those imagined lines of division in society that are about a sense of control over what matters, what is valuable or worthy of protection or not (which can be jobs in the steel industry, as much as a form of entertainment, or lifestyle). So, it is also very much a matter of who calls the cultural shots, of who has control over cultural and social codes. These codes are not separate from economic choices, and neither are their symbols.[1] In a speech in Thors in south-east France, Jordan Bardella, who led the Rassemblement National European election list, gave a speech that illustrates this merging of the cultural and the economic. He started with the latest French

---

1. This is why the debates about whether recent instances of populist mobilization (the election of Donald Trump or the vote in favour of Brexit) are about economics *or* culture completely miss the point: it is about how economics *fashion* culture, and vice-versa. An excellent article that explores the relationship between these attitudes is Georgiadou, Rori & Roumanias 2018.

census numbers and French birth rate; and swiftly noted that the birth rate was down: "cribs remain empty" he said. But, he noted, the population of the country had increased. "But I'm sure you all have some idea of how this has happened. Don't you?" he teased. "Of course, it is massive immigration and an elite that is all in favour of it. That doesn't care about your low wages or despair. That doesn't give a damn that your life is going to the dogs". Here the distinction between economic, social and cultural elites is left quite hazy – they are all rolled into one. Above all, the impact of that elite is economic, cultural and extremely personal.[2]

But the use of the divide between the people and the elite, whilst crucial, is complex. More so than discussions generally allow. It is not enough to be critical of elites; most politicians run against the status quo, and that is not enough to make them populist, otherwise everyone is (and it is that slippery tendency that sees unscrupulous observers label anyone. from France's Emmanuel Macron to Bernie Sanders in the US, a populist). Jan Werner Muller makes this point effectively by going a little further:

> In addition to being anti-elitist, populists are always *antiplural-ist*. Populists claim that they, and they alone, represent people [...] The claim to exclusive representation is not an empirical one; it is always distinctly *moral*. When running for office, populists portray their political competitors as part of the immoral, corrupt elite; when ruling, they refuse to recognize any opposition as legitimate (Muller 2017: 4; emphasis in the original).

This moral dimension is in part what makes populist leaders or positions so difficult to counter: their opponent is not merely an opponent to be argued with, they are an enemy to be annihilated; because the duty of morality is to vanquish immorality. The moral dimension of the concept of the people is crucial. And it goes perhaps even further than Muller points out. While some have argued that Muller's take on the morality of the concept makes his stance too polemical, this seems to miss the point (see Stavrakakis & Jager 2018): in populist politics, the people are conceived of as a moral entity because its claims are rooted in moral claims. These are not just accusations about the opposition's lack of probity or

---

2. Jordan Bardella, RN public meeting in Thors (Vaucluse), 19 January 2019.

moral compass (which are pervasive in any adversarial politics since, after all, most parties would be arguing that theirs is a blueprint to the best and most just vision of society); but in populism the people are granted a moral claim simply by virtue (literally) of who they are. What populists outline as the commonality of the people – what makes the people, "The People" – from Poujade to Salvini, from Wilders to Trump, from Mélenchon to Beppe Grillo – is that they have an innate sense of what is right and what is just. This is in part why so much populist politics will short-circuit discussion or examination: because the people's preferences are innate. And because they are innate, they are just and cannot be argued with.

At the heart of populism's vision of the people is that of a moral order that is guaranteed by this intrinsic connection between the people and their sense of what is morally and obviously right. The notion of common sense complements this moral understanding of the people. Common sense is one of those important contextual concepts: it is what gives the people their inalienable legitimacy to govern themselves. In the popular imagination it is the crucial quality that sets the people apart from the elite. They have it, they have the capacity to instinctively know what is right and what is effective. This means that common sense is also a moral attribute. No acquired knowledge or "book smarts" can replace it.

Finally, common sense posits a fundamental quality of the people which is their capacity to understand each other almost wordlessly. This is a politics that is based on the ideal of being wordlessly understood by those who surround you because common sense is, well, common – as in "shared". And because it is instinctive as opposed to intellectually developed, it has one added nifty quality: it can allow you to immediately recognize those who are part of "the people". Common sense is the secret decoder ring of populism. We will come back to the centrality of this immediacy of understanding in populist politics.

What about leadership?

One question that often comes up is that of the status of the leader: how can the concept of the people be a credible idea to mobilize supporters when it is so clear that many of their leaders are far removed, socially, from ordinary people? Two things are worth saying here. The first is that countless conversations and discussion groups with populist party supporters suggests that, as voters and political subjects, they are either entirely unbothered by the contradiction, or in fact oblivious to it, because someone is, at last, speaking in their name, with their words, about their views and preferences. This disjunction simply does not matter. But it never has, for any ideology: socialist leaders were generally well-educated career-politicians and conservatives could be drawn (occasionally!) from more modest backgrounds. The populist claims about speaking in the name of ordinary people are believable on a different and more important level: namely, a moral level. "I share your outrage" is all that is needed. This becomes even more obvious in later populist movements and parties.

Are populist's people really all of the people?

Another issue that is often raised is whether the centrality of the people is real, or credible, since populists are only speaking for a section of the population, and sometimes only a minority of heavily disgruntled voters. Trying to counter populist politics by "catching it out" on such counterfactuals seems utterly useless. Trying to understand populist politics as working *despite* such political sleights of hand is entirely missing the point. The point of an ideology is not to be true, but to be believable. And whether or not it is believable, depends on whether it is able to mobilize resentment, and grievances, but also myths and the popular imagination. It is enough for populist leaders to create an imagined community of ordinary people. Much as it was enough for socialism to mobilize solidarity across the globe for an imagined international working class. Whether or not either group is truly a majority (paradoxically for movements who often advocate rule by blunt majoritarianism), does not necessarily matter. Who actually constitutes this community and whether it is entirely rallying behind the movement in question is secondary. There may be more reality to the Occupy movement's claim to be the 99 per cent than to populism's "real people". But, again, it doesn't matter because the way in which populism defines the real people is simply 100 per cent of those who want to be The People. Even if they are only 20 per cent of voters. The "people" we are talking about here are an imagined entity; and the populist leader, and their programme, allows it to imagine itself. Perhaps even to reveal itself to others: a key point in shaping and encouraging a new consensus. In contemporary populisms, in fact, the leaders and the parties do not only *create* this imagined community, they *reveal* it as the new consensus to the rest of society.[3]

One point is worth stressing here, however. Populists – politicians and voters – are not oblivious to the numbers; far from it. Their love of a good referendum is proof of that. Referendums create the perfect opportunity to reveal the new consensus, to unveil the will of the people. Even if in fact it is simply measuring something else. In the case of the UK referendum on leaving the European Union in 2016, the fact that the Leave campaign won with 52 per cent of the vote (17.4 million people) was the cornerstone of all arguments and negotiations. These are not all of the people (after all 16 million voted to remain in the EU), but the argument is that those 17.4 million are the "real" people; they are the real nation. The others are the enemy.

Do left and right populism share the same vision of the people?

There is one final distinction that often gets elided, but is worthy of some attention, and that is the differing conceptions of "the people" that underpin right and left populisms. This is a crucial issue. One of populism's key facets is that it can appear on either side of the political spectrum. A claim often made by populists is that they cut across left and right because – or so the populist story goes – the distinction between the two is an artificial distraction invented by elites to keep the people divided. "But we are above such partisan divisions; we are in favour of the people" is a recurring theme in populist politics. The point is to distance one's party or movement, from "the system". There is almost no populist party in Europe that hasn't at one point adopted a version of the slogan "neither right nor left – for the people" (and very distinct from the "*both* left *and* right" stance of coalitions or centrists that are cast by

---

3. The unspoken argument is often actually remarkably close to what socialists once called false consciousness, which suggested that a great number of people were not yet aware of their true interests (this explained why all working-class people did not vote for working-class parties, because they suffered from false consciousness). The populists in many respects work on the same principle: once the new consensus is revealed then the real people would rally. They would be, as the current alt-right lingo puts it, "woke".

populists as the very proof of the elite stitch-up they denounce). There is a strong possibility, not that the populists are right – in that they are rarely truly beyond the right/left distinction – but that the distinction is not a particularly relevant feature of populism. Yet there is one instance in which this distinction matters and that is in how they define the people, because it impacts on their views on immigration and nativism.

A number of definitions, including Mudde's, contain an attempt to define the people as imagined by populists by referring to the fact that what populists privilege above all is the people's "collective will". Mudde even refers to the "general will" (or "*volonté générale*" to use Rousseau's term). This is useful to remind us that we are dealing with a holistic, organic – almost metaphysical – conception of the people. But the use of a rather controversial and multi-form expression tends to obscure that fundamental distinction between the will of the people (as the will of the majority), and the will of the people, as conceived of by Rousseau, as "the sum of the differences of everyone's private interests", which suggests a more minimal agreement based on an agreed lowest common denominator, rather than the potentially oppressive act of a numerical majority, regardless of the will and preferences of others (Kain 1990: 316–7).

Left populism is – generally – rooted in a conception of the general will that posits each citizen as bearing inalienable (human) rights worthy of collective protection (not to be confused with individualism); the people are the expression of the collective will of sovereign citizens. The collectivism, in other words, is a choice, although it can sometimes feel no less oppressive for that. Right-wing populism, on the other hand, grounds its general will in something far more organic: there is no metaphysical understanding of the transformation of distinct citizens into a collective that *chooses* to abide by a collectively agreed set of laws. There is only a belief in an existing mass that is bound together organically. Hence the, initial, overwhelming rejection by right-wing populists of the concept of human rights.[4]

This is an important distinction, not because it means that left-wing populists are any less pernicious to representative institutions than

---

4. Initial because some populists, such as Geert Wilders in the Netherlands, but also Marine Le Pen in France have belatedly taken to those as a means of attacking Islam. Islam is then decried as violating, for example, the human rights of women.

right-wing populists, but because it means that left-wing populists are more immune from nativism and nativity foibles. In other words, while both sides fetishize the notion of the people in ways that allow it to mount an attack on established elites as they imagine them, and on the basis of a fundamental betrayal of the people, their lines of attack will differ. For left-wing populists, the notion of betrayal need not be rooted in the organic, racial, ethnic homogeneity of the people; it will be enough that they are bearers of shared fundamental rights that are being undermined by the elite (although how these shared rights are interpreted and safeguarded by left-wing populists is no less problematic). This gives rise to demands for direct democracy, wholesale attacks on institutions, and conspiracy theories – much as it would on the right. But for right-wing populists the betrayal of the elite will take place against a group that imagines itself as a natural and often homogenous entity, not a politically constructed one.

This explains why for right-wing populists the idea of the nation plays such a powerful role. Although in right-wing populism the nation can often be rooted in blood-ties (rather than in territorial or institutional allegiance) the nation is also conceived of as cultural community based on an intuitive conception of "culture" – is so intuitive in fact, that it is, in effect, "un-absorbable" by those who are not naturally "of it"; which is why right-wing populism despite a detour via culture, ends up in nativist territory. Although seldom based strictly on race, lineage matters: a connection to the people and the nation that is ancestral and gives the individual the capacity to connect instinctively to the values of the nation and of the others around him or her is a crucial attribute. Left-wing populism draws on this notion of cultural homogeneity as well: hard-working, ordinary people whose interests are shaped by shared experiences that come to be inscribed in the collective, just as surely as ethnicity is inscribed in DNA. This means that xenophobia is also an adjacent concept; it serves to strengthen the boundaries of the real people against the other. It can be racially defined, but also culturally. So it is a broad rejection of the other who is beyond the boundaries of shared common sense, and therefore suspect. This explains the paramount role that immigration – reliant on permeability and adaptation – plays as a policy theme for all populists.

Betrayal

A story of betrayal is the second key component of the populist ideas core. The betrayal by the elite – and especially those in elected positions of power – of ordinary people, is the teleological myth that fuels populism. The story is one of usurpation: the accusation is not of a wresting of power by coup, or even an acquiring of power by rigged vote or corruption, or even for that matter the transmission of power and privilege through family (which is often acceptable to right-wing populists who see in it the affirmation of a naturally ordered society). No, it is the winning of power by legal and democratic means with the support of the people and in their name, only to develop (or reveal) different intentions once in power and betray those who trusted them. The accusation – and the story of the betrayal – is that this elite develops a greater sense of allegiance with its own members than with either the people or the nation. This "defection" of representatives to "the other side" as a constitutive feature of politics seems quite specific to populism and fuels the "broken promises" rhetoric.

The idea that members of the various elite groups have more in common with one another than with the people they are there to represent is rooted in a conception of professional politics as something that instantly corrupts, and as a lure, and is evidence of the weak will of those who govern through these means. By virtue (or vice) of becoming a part of the elite, of becoming "a professional", the politician is corrupted in her or his ethics and becomes, at best, useless to the people, and at worst its enemy. Hence the rejection of professional politics – as the abdication of authenticity – the calls to "drain the swamp", and, ultimately, the fundamental instability of populist parties, forever torn between running for power (and becoming part of the swamp) or storming the citadel but never accessing the real levers of change. It is a deeply paradoxical and tragic situation. But the tragedy feeds the sense of injustice and betrayal.

And it is in that defection of the elected politician, or the upstart intellectual, or the liberal convert that populism draws its powerful story of betrayal. At the heart of populist politics lies the persistent, relentless idea of a broken democratic promise, a betrayal of the people (and, most often, the lost honour of the nation). You can find it across the board in all of these movements that we term "populist" – from Trump to Le Pen (both of them), from the AfD to the Five Star Movement.

The betrayal goes hand in hand with two other important ideas in the pantheon of populist ideas: conspiracy and decline. The accusations of corruption specify the nature of the betrayal – they give it colour, context, reality; and the betrayal by elites is often portrayed as a conspiracy, and the latter are rife in populist stories.[5] Second, a foundational and acute sense of the nation's decline coupled with great nostalgia is part of this cluster. While this is not one of the core ideas – to the extent say, that it would be core to Conservatism – it is nevertheless an idea that plays an important role. Indeed, the kind of conception of the nation and the betrayal of the democratic promise that we find at the heart of populism rests on an acute sense of both the nation's rise and fall: the decline against which populism exhorts its followers to fight, is about both a vision of the past, as well as a vision of place. Place both as a geographical instance, but also a reference to one's secure sense of place in society. Nostalgia takes different forms; for right-wing populism this nostalgia is about a loss of the sense of greatness: the pervasive feeling that "our finest hour" is always in the past. For left-wing populists, the longing and nostalgia are often about a sense of loss of innocence, or loss of purity. Not so much past greatness, as past innocence and simplicity. For both, it gets expressed through a longing for stable hierarchies, well-defined roles and clear-cut, fixed identities – be they work, gender, or ethnic identities.

Democracy

The third main ingredient of populism is a devotion to, in fact a fetishization of, democracy. We have alluded to this before: democracy is not just populism's "theatre of operations", it also plays a fundamental role in the populist world view and call to action. As a reference point, democracy can be attractive because, in its most basic and odious form – its strictly majoritarian, and sometimes direct, form – it can be used

---

5. See Taguieff 2005; Morris & Kreko 2014. See also http://counterpoint.uk.com/trust-and-conspiracy-theories/ and http://counterpoint.uk.com/the-psychology-of-conspiracy-theory/ (accessed 19 March 2019).

to quash dissent and marginalize minorities, and by the same token validate both the will of the people and its existence. Majoritarian democracy can be a very swift way of sifting the "real" people from the others. Populist-tabloid Brexit rhetoric that accused the UK judiciary of being "enemies of the people"[6] in response to a Supreme Court ruling that granted the British Parliament a meaningful vote on the Brexit deal, is an excellent example. The people, the nation, and the majority are intrinsically linked, indeed they are often fantasized as one.

But democracy also plays a different role: it acts as a reliable supplier of betrayal. Democracy promises access and voice and so easily feeds the fantasy of betrayal, because by definition a democratic system will translate into the will of some over others and therefore the potential to use a very democratic language to call into question the result. This is why populism can really ever only exist in contexts where there is at least a semblance of democracy or emerging democracy: because democracy is both the aim, but also the condition in which the betrayal necessary to populism's story can occur. Authoritarian regimes on the other hand, are scant on promises of voice. They rarely raise anybody's hopes that they will be heard or listened to. Even when they make promises (of protection or prosperity) they do not make promises about the value of individual and collective voices being taken into account. Without the oxygen of that promise about the process, there can be no populism, because there can be no betrayal.

Authenticity

So far, the ideas we have evoked should come as no surprise. But there is a key idea at the heart of populism that never quite gets the attention it deserves, and that is the idea of authenticity. Yet, arguably, authenticity might be the idea that holds it all together, and more to the point, that has allowed populism to exert such influence in recent decades. If democracy promises access and voice, authenticity promises genuine relationships. And, by definition, a deeply relational politics.

Authenticity is a vastly undervalued idea that is only now rising to the top of discussion lists. Generally, authenticity has been held as an

---

6. *Daily Mail*, front-page headline, 4 November 2016.

unalloyed positive. I return to authenticity's dual nature in the conclusion. However, in various types of populisms it performs a specific set of functions. Authenticity is first and foremost a concept that allows for a politics rooted in instinct rather than reason. It is useful (1) to brand all others as hypocrites; (2) as a blanket excuse to speak one's mind in ways that are as disruptive as possible, unbounded by received social and political norms; and (3) to make good on the populist claim that instinct and common sense trump reason and strategy. In this last respect, it is a gateway to the disruption that populists seek

Populism does not pit emotions against reason, as is so often argued (that tired trope about the head and the heart). But rather reason (which we know is a mix of rationality and emotion)[7] on the one hand, against instinct on the other. So, this is not as the cliché often goes, a politics that pits emotions against rationality; but rather one that pits instinct against the head and the heart. Populism is a politics of the gut. And claims to authenticity are populism's way of legitimizing that politics of the gut.

For starters, such claims to authenticity go a long way toward justifying all manner of careless pronouncements since expressing your "true, spontaneous self" cannot be held against you. Paradoxically, authenticity is also a trump card (no pun intended) that can be played when caught in a lie – lying and covering up is what real humans do. Claims to authenticity can grant the most disingenuous behaviour a measure of sincerity (and so there is an interesting link between lying and authenticity; one that populism exploits relentlessly). And, short of producing the impression of sincerity, this kind of bombastic authenticity achieved through lying is often worn as a badge of "chuzpah" – a willingness to game the system shamelessly and designed to highlight the arcane morality and stupidity of the person, or institution, being deceived. (The Rassemblement National's attitude to being caught using European Parliament funds for domestic party purposes is a good case in point; being accused and caught causes no embarrassment whatsoever: the RN was simply "playing" a silly institution too caught up in its precious rules and regulations; they, the RN, on the other hand, are real people trying to get things done.) It is this recourse to authenticity that can reconcile the apparent contradictions of populism: claiming

7. See, for example, just to name a few, Kahneman 2011; Marcus 2002; Westen 2007; Harmon-Jones & Winkeman 2007.

to be honest and being caught lying, claiming to understand the people and not necessarily acting in their best interest. There is always the possibility of redeeming one's self by admitting to being no more than an ordinary, authentic human being prone to messing up. Or simply smarter than those people or institutions who deserve to be outwitted.

Second, the corollary to all this, of course, is that every other form of politics can be cast as either manipulative or hypocritical, or both. Any curb on this political instinct is depicted as an attempt to silence verity and derail common sense. The attacks on political correctness (generally characterized as an over-intellectualization, or over-moralization of straightforward matters by bleeding-heart liberals or puritans, both accused of hypocrisy) are one expression of this core belief.

Perhaps the most important function performed by the idea of authenticity in the populist cluster of ideas is to connect to the people's experience. Claims to authenticity enable populist discourse to contrast the unmediated natural intelligence or instinct of the people (who are authentic) with the acquired knowledge, book-learning, and (untrustworthy) sophistication of the elite. In this populist world view, anyone's intimation that an issue might not be clear cut, or that hesitating might be understandable given the issue's complexity, are all taken as symptomatic of a weakness of character, and of potential corruptibility: problems need to be approached with common sense and pragmatism, and solutions should be obvious to those who have the interests of the people at heart. Invoking complexity, is usually seen as an attempt to bamboozle the people. Claims to "being right" must be the product of instinct, or they are not to be trusted. There is no room for grey areas. So, for example, emancipating one's self from the community of the nation (through travel, curiosity, hybridity and dual identities) necessarily amounts to a rejection of the natural, unbroken, and unspoken link to the people.

This explains why another related set of ideas crops up regularly in discussions about populism, but also in populist manifestos: directness, immediacy and transparency. In terms of directness, we are not just talking about forms of direct democracy like referendums, but also references to that direct, wordless understanding between the members of the same community, or between the leader and his or her followers (that we alluded to earlier on), or the chosen means of expression by the leader (straight-talking, often via a face-to-face simulacrum as allowed by social media). The point of this emphasis on directness is, first, that nothing will stand between the people and the expression of their will – so that excludes representative institutions. Second, directness connects to the role of common sense and the idea of a shared nature that needs no explaining – just displaying.

Immediacy refers to populism's relentless insistence that the people should make their minds up quickly, almost instantaneously; but also that their decision-makers should deliver solutions or resolve problems also instantaneously. In other words, the very opposite of what complexity might require, and in some respects a denial of the very existence of complexity. As for transparency, it is the enabler of authenticity. Transparency creates the possibility of an authentic politics: the people reveal themselves and are transparent and readable to each other; their leaders reveal themselves to the people. And the people as a whole comes into being.

So authenticity is the great "activator" of the democracy that populists call for: it creates the conditions whereby the people recognize each other and it creates both the possibility of avoiding betrayal as well as enabling the wordless understanding and recognition that populism depends upon to sort the people from the elite. In these acts of readability and recognition, authenticity plays a crucial role because it is relational. It posits the framework through which leaders are recognized as such, but also the mechanism through which the people become themselves. Authenticity is intrinsic to populism because it posits the kind of political relationship that needs to be achieved, and the relationship is an end in itself.

Finally, going a little further, authenticity, as conceived of in populist politics, can provide a way to deal with shame and humiliation. Speaking outrageous untruths, pretending to believe them, but also speaking truth outrageously, voicing opinions that are at the very limit of taboo, all of this is about triumphing over shame – by speaking. Conquering the perceived humiliation inflicted by the elite by being, literally, shameless. Whether this is the perceived, collective humiliation of being relegated to the status of medium-sized power; or the individually perceived humiliation of not having the right educational credentials, or cultural reference points. All of these can be temporarily addressed, or rather eclipsed, by outrageously human bad behaviour. In this respect, authenticity is also what "ups the ante"; it is what accounts for the sense of a spiral that lead from insinuation, to accusation, to half-truth, to lie, to enormous lie, and finally, to conspiracy theory.[8]

In the previous chapter I wrote about our puzzlement vis-á-vis the quality of our political moment. The next chapters are designed in part to illustrate that the ideas across our case studies are familiar ideas, but what changes their impact, and grants the populist moment its quality, is the license that authenticity grants with respect to their use. In this respect, the value of authenticity and the claims to it are the secret ingredient that hold populism together as an ideological project. Authenticity turns the thin-centred ideology into a powerful one.

So, who is out?

Before moving to the next part of the discussion, it is worth drawing a couple of conclusions from these core ideas. These conclusions allow us to eliminate a few parties and leaders from the current populist pantheon. I regularly come across references to Bernie Sanders and to Jeremy Corbyn as populists. Neither of them fits the bill under the ideas outlined above (and this is not a case of "the people I like cannot be populists", because it would only apply to one of them). Neither of them puts all elites in the same bag: they both focus quite specifically on financial elites and on the economic damage that such elites are inflicting on ordinary people; and neither of them reduces their political opponent to the status of enemy. In both cases we seem to be confronted with quite mainstream political projects: one socialist (in the case of Corbyn), and the other perhaps best described as social democratic (in the case of Sanders).

Above all, neither leader, neither movement, draws any strength from the notion of a people that is in any way homogenous, or in any way morally superior, or more deserving than others. In fact, there are very few appeals to "the people" but rather, to "ordinary citizens" – a

---

8. But it is also what accounts for the almost inevitable one-upmanship between parties and their leaders. The quest to be "even more" authentic, and in many cases even more outrageous than others (in part, sometimes, just to remain audible) accounts for dynamics and the self-fulfilling prophecies of populism. Those parties and those politicians who choose not to adopt that style need to be very astute indeed to remain in the race.

distinction that displays respect for existing institutions (as opposed to populism's suspicion of them). Furthermore, the appeals are not to common sense, or an innate sense of entitlement, but to an elaborate social justice system based on redistribution and human rights. Both offer radically alternative views to what is the current governmental offer in the UK and the United States, but neither counts as populist. This impression is reinforced further when contrasted with the case of France's Jean-Luc Mélenchon, who is also on the left (and formerly affiliated to the French Socialist Party) but whose ideas nevertheless fall squarely into the populist category. What makes him different? Certainly his relentless use of "the people", but also his recurrent calls for an abolition of current political institutions, and his calls for absolute popular sovereignty.

This is a good place to address the case studies that follow. In the next few chapters I want to examine four countries (France, the Netherlands, Italy and the UK) that have been some of the important national contexts in which western European populism has developed. First, whilst dissimilar in a number of ways (historical trajectory, traditions of electoral behaviour, political cultures, political institutions) these cases nevertheless share a number of attributes that make them particularly interesting for comparative purposes: all of them are prosperous, technologically advanced, liberal polities with large-scale systems of social protection; and all of them have been subject recently to waves (of different types) of migration. Second, they all seem busy dismantling their own success. They are in some ways, democracies that allow us to explore the link between democracy and its dark shadow most vividly. Seventy years of uninterrupted peace and sustained prosperity are giving way to sustained assaults against those institutions that made them possible. In some ways my interest is not terribly different from that of Avner Offer who, in *The Challenge of Affluence*, explores why those very institutions that made prosperity possible (work, restraint and effort) are those that create its fragility (Offer 2007). Authenticity, so intrinsic to the Enlightenment project, but also more narrowly to democratic life, is also a victim of its own success – granting populism the means to challenge the foundations of the representative democratic edifice.

Finally, these four cases serve to illustrate both the core of populist ideas, as well as its evolution. They can be read as western European populism's evolutionary spiral in which we can discern both a stable

DNA, and the effects of history and events on this DNA. So while the appeal to the people, the stories of betrayal, the moral claims, and the bid for a politics of authenticity are detectable throughout, some traits become more marked over generations, while others fade. The French case study is archetypal of populism's gradual evolution away from fascism and traditional nationalism under the impetus of the postwar status quo; the Dutch case study is emblematic of what comes next: the collision between national politics and globalization (and globalization's main symbol: mass migration); Italy builds on these developments and is paradigmatic of the resulting transformation between leadership and media in the context of a growing revolt against the political mainstream as it emerges from the end of the Cold War. At this juncture (and it is not over yet), the UK comes across as a kind of apogee of populist politics – such is the symbol of a politics dictated by a blunt referendum, the marginalization of a large minority, the accusations of betrayal and the sweeping rejection of all things globalized or plural.

All of these cases build on one another in a kind of spiral fuelled by the fundamental transformations unleashed by global interdependence, and accelerated by Digital. But they also feed off each other as they overlap in a kind of ideological rippling. They exhibit similarities with each other and with other cases to which I refer. In this respect the four cases are both paradigmatic as well as a set of lenses through which to interpret the many cases of populism in the rest of the world. They help us tell a rather universal story about populism: its ideational roots, the role of its leaders, its growth and spread, and the particular way in which across the board populism has found itself confronted with a changing political subject that has become increasingly susceptible to its siren song of populist politics.

3

The prototype: France

Starting with Jean-Marie Le Pen may seem strange. After all he is no longer leader of the Front National (which is no longer called the Front National), he is an elderly man and his political career is over. And yet, it all starts with Jean-Marie Le Pen. When Le Pen formed the FN the Second World War had been over for less than 30 years. It was 1972 in fact, the last gasp of the immediate postwar era. It was the end of the boom years (the "thirty glorious ones" as the French refer to them) and just one year before the oil shock of 1973, which would mark the end of Europe's most prosperous era.

The FN would come to provide the bridge between the old extreme right (still tainted by Nazism and fascism) and the new right-wing populism of the twenty-first century. By 2002, Le Pen had made it all the way to the second round of the French presidential elections (narrowly beating Socialist candidate Lionel Jospin to second place with 16.86% of the vote – Jospin had scored 16.18%). It took 30 years, but in those three decades Le Pen rewrote the gamebook for challenger parties on the right and shaped contemporary populism. In Le Pen's formulations and behaviour we can detect the beginnings of a powerful appeal to transparency and to a new form of authentic politics.

The Front national: prototyping contemporary populism

The year 1972 was not Le Pen's first foray into politics. After a brief stint in the National Assembly (in 1956 as an MP for Pierre Poujade's Union de Défense des Commerçants et des Artisans (UDCA) – an early populist precursor), Le Pen momentarily faded from view and, in 1962, the new, Fifth Republic swept away the relics of the Fourth and its institutions were kind to no one but its Gaullist architects. The next few years would bear the hallmarks of this deep political transformation: the Algerian war, decolonization, the rise of Gaullism and its struggle to impose order on the French party system. De Gaulle opened up France, but he was a man of his time: government's role was to rein in chaos. And he was a French statesman: the state's role was to protect and control. De Gaulle, amongst other things, was trying to accomplish two tasks that might seem contradictory: to drag France into modernity on the one hand (motorways, supermarkets, technocratic government, freedom for France's former colonies, and votes for women); while simultaneously fixing the boundaries of politics and of the nation (controlling the media, engineering a new type of party system and establishing a new type of leadership fit for twentieth century France). When Le Pen did re-emerge, in the early 1970s, it was in part to begin to take advantage of the latter, and systematically undermine the former. Le Pen cracked the code of the Fifth Republic and worked the system in order to subvert it (see Fieschi 2004).

Through Poujade and his party, Le Pen had developed his distaste for modernity: the UDCA was a movement of the provincial petty-bourgeoisie against the growing challenge of large suppliers and a tax system that did little for them. Indeed, in many ways Poujadism was a basic tax revolt dressed up as political rebellion.[1] Against the backdrop of the Fourth Republic's twilight years, the UDCA and its 400,000 members were the last gasps of an order forever annihilated by the Second World War, and buried by de Gaulle, but whose protagonists, even with their old habitat in tatters, attempted one final assault on modernity. On his return from Algeria, Le Pen flirted with a number of hard-right political options. Having fought in the Organisation Armée Secrète (OAS) against Algerian independence, his stance was critical of de Gaulle and infused with a deep sense of France's marginalization as a superpower.

There is no underestimating the role that this imagined, slighted, diminished France played in the conception of the FN: the party was driven by the idea of recapturing glory, and halting both political decline and moral decadence, and most right-wing populists have not moved very far from this. This is not simply a question of rhetoric, it drove

---

1. Le Pen often recounted that when he met Poujade in 1955, the latter said to him "you will be a tricolour planted on the cash-registers of France".

the conception of the party, its political aims and its strategy. In many respects it still does, and to some extent Marine Le Pen still straddles her father's heritage and the demands of the present uneasily. Hence the somewhat roller-coaster quality of her popularity and political successes.

In 1972 Le Pen's job was to federate a disparate crew made up of traditional counter-revolutionaries (yes, even in 1972, some found the French Revolution and its subsequent Republics illegitimate), anti-Semites, anti-communists, old-style Catholics, revisionists, colonialists, anti-Gaullists, violent nationalists and straggling neo-Nazis and neo-Fascists. A really nice bunch. To do this, Le Pen surrounded himself with various figures who could keep the different factions in check and give them just enough attention to keep them in line, but no so much as to embolden them.[2]

Strategically, the aim was to move away from the violent and counter-productive tactics of the 1960s and adapt to the requirements of de Gaulle's Fifth Republican, ballot-box imperative: it was to create an actual party, rather than to remain a movement that was constantly in danger of self-combusting, and/or being outlawed as a result of its guerrilla tactics. This meant elaborating a programme, a set of policy-lines, and harnessing the energy and assorted resentments of these various gangs, all for electoral gain. It is worth highlighting just how isolated the FN was at its inception: both dominant parties (the Gaullists and the Communists) were enemies; and in his strategic determination to break with far-right groups and far-right doctrine, Le Pen made the FN an island. What follows is a brief portrait of the kinds of ideas that Le Pen brought to this endeavour. They are important because they serve as a kind of foundational ideas matrix for populists to come. Through Le Pen we can see the emergence of key ideas that have turned populism into the powerful ideology that it is today. We can see an uneasy truce (still at play but less obviously so) between traditional nationalism and the re-emergence of a new conception of the people; a tug of war between the nostalgia for pre-revolutionary France and the necessary conversion to democracy and to the Republic; and above all we can see the first signs of populism's jiu-jitsu move that was to capture the Enlightenment's reverence for authenticity and turn it against its values.

2. On the creation of the FN, one of the best accounts is in Gombin 2016.

An ideas blueprint for twenty-first-century European populism

A quick precis of Le Pen's key ideas gives us a good sense both of the foundational role they play in the forging of a European populist world view, but also helps us keep track of the evolution that takes place.

The nation and the people

One of the few times in which I found myself in Le Pen's study – as he reflected and spun me yet another yarn about his humble beginnings (this time the story about his father was that he had been killed by the Germans – which is not an outright lie – and his body found on the beach with the eyes gouged out – which is an outright lie) – he began to talk about his vision of France, and a clear sense of his understanding of the nation came through.

He kept repeating a sentence, which was to stick with me for a long time afterwards: "the presence of France upon the seas". The image was a powerful one, looking out as we were over Paris, surrounded by min-iature boat replicas; my eye constantly caught by one sailing ornament or another. The expression evoked an almost divine permanence, a tri-umph of national will over sheer physical impossibility: a nation stand-ing atop the churning sea. But also, a nation that naturally knew how to rule them.[3] And, of course, the timelessness evoked by the incredible feat of steadfastness. For Le Pen, the nation was the ultimate weapon against potential chaos.

The appeal to the nation and the deep connection to nationalism were at the heart of Le Pen's FN and underpinned all of the party's other aspects. This was core then, and it is still core now. But that nation is inseparable from its people: it is both nothing without them, and so much more than the sum of them. And over time, Le Pen would begin to privilege the people over the nation. "The people" – organic but also, crucially, quantifiable – were the way to connect to the democratic bal-lot, and the institutions of the fifth Republic.

---

3. In French, "*la presence de la France sur les mers*" has an added ring. The definite article "*la*" emphasizes the feminine qualities of the nation (over the more masculine ones of the state) and whilst there is a vulnerability of the singular, single nation against the many, plural seas, there is also a sense of natural fit here between the ruler and the ruled.

The dividing line became starker and starker: from the election posters ("Le Pen, Le Peuple") to his frequent and endless speeches, Jean-Marie Le Pen did not miss an opportunity to attack "establishment politicians", to denounce "the huge gap between the people and its so-called representatives" as well as "that oligarchy" that "highjacks" institutions for its own interests. The "apparatchik cast", hell-bent on its "privileges", "disconnected from the people about whose aspirations it has no idea about", became the privileged scapegoat of Le Pen's rhetoric from the get-go. He went on to draw a distinction between the "false elite" (in power but illegitimate) and the "real elite" – those who "have the courage to say things and do things", and that "the French people, naturally endowed with political common sense, recognise instinctively".[4] This was a first, distinct step away from the far-right tradition and toward populism.

And it is a major distinction: that while far-right themes and discourses (inspired by nationalism) endow the people with formidable powers, populism singles out the ordinariness of the people: the extraordinary powers come from ordinary common sense. There is no promise of a great rebirth because of magical national qualities or a violent renewal in blood and violence (in the way that fascism promises: see Griffin 1993), there is simply the promise of getting rid of a treasonous and decadent elite (much as in fascism) but by re-becoming one's self: special because authentic, and authentically ordinary.

The (natural) order of things

The permanent analogy between the nation and the family is something that has remained a dominant theme for the FN. In this respect, "Montretout", the Le Pen family home, is worth a quick mention as the scene of the Le Pen family saga. In many respects the home and its grounds serve as a microcosm of the political world as imagined by Le Pen.[5]

---

4. Various party meetings.
5. In Montretout Le Pen hosted the relics of France's far right and emerging new right; but also, minor stars and celebrities (as well as a few rather larger stars such as the actor Alain Delon). It was a stage for power-plays and for repeated demonstrations of Le Pen's pull. In many ways it was, quite literally, a salon. Albeit not of a very

Montretout was also the scene of many a break-up: first and fore-most, from his first wife, Pierrette, who slammed the door of the con-jugal home one evening in 1987. As an act of rebellion, she made off with Jean-Marie's best glass eye, but forgot the urn containing her mother's ashes; the protracted negotiation over these two objects that followed as part of the divorce proceedings would not be out of place in one of the more outrageous Feydeau farces.[6] More to the point, and entertainment value aside, such antics are symptomatic of the kind of power-plays that underpin all family relationship chez les Le Pen. In 1998, in the aftermath of the split within the FN, Marie-Caroline Le Pen, the eldest daughter, also left Montretout since she and her husband had sided with Bruno Mégret, Le Pen's challenger. Finally, in 2014, in the final throes of her very public split from her father, Marine left the family home. None of these women chose to go quietly; there is, and was, much drama involved.

Over the years, Montretout became the embodiment of Le Pen's conception of politics. Long before there was talk of "Fortress Europe", the driving idea in Le Pen's political repertoire was fortress France. If de Gaulle had a certain vision of France as a heroic damsel in perma-nent distress, then Le Pen's vision of France was decidedly more Joan of Arc: recovering France from various forms of domination was the mis-sion; betrayed by its own, but standing strong until those enemies from within were thwarted, the traitors Le Pen was forever guarding against. He remains the last guardian of the fortress under siege.

But more than that, Montretout was also the site of the tragic betrayal of natural hierarchies (by his wife and then his son-in-law and finally two of his three daughters). His well-known quip that "I love my daugh-ter (or my family) more than my friends, my friends more than my neighbours, my neighbours more than my fellow country-men, and my fellow-country men more than Europeans"[7] is a good illustration of the immutable, natural organic order of things: Allegiances start with the family and move in concentric circles of declining commitment and

---

intellectual kind. Above all this salon was to be a concentrate of what mattered in French society and of what might bring about the change Le Pen sought and the showcase for Le Pen as leader of this clan.

6. Legend, or rather documented gossip, has it that the objects in question were later exchanged by the parties' respective lawyers somewhere in the woods outside Paris. Feydeau meets Le Carre.

7. Jean-Marie Le Pen, 9 December 2006.

intensity; the appeal in this formulation is to something we might call "sentimental common sense", that it is sentimentally natural (and therefore right) to see it this way. This would be brought into relief when he fell out with his daughter Marine in 2011 and aligned himself with his grand-daughter Marion. All in the family, just one rung down. It is through this conception of the family as the primary building block – a microcosm – of society that the clannish aspects of the Le Pen saga are recast by Le Pen from corruption and nepotism into a coherent vision of politics.

Betrayal and decline

This natural order of things, so prized by Le Pen and his populist emulators, is what was initially challenged by the Republican order and, later, by the party system. For Le Pen, the beginning of decline is 1789 with a revolution that creates parties, factions and divisions that, according to him, artificially divide the French nation by imposing a non-natural hierarchy on people's natural values and inclinations. Indeed, at its beginnings, the FN, was markedly, relentlessly, critical of the Republic and of the 1789 revolution that marks its birth. Behind this revulsion toward the Republic (something that does ebb over time as evidenced by Marine Le Pen's defence of republican values) lurked a number of things. Some of them were purely tactical, like wanting to include every, last possible supporter, including any residual monarchists (as this strand of politics becomes increasingly "niche", attacks on the revolution become less frequent). But some of the anti-Republican springs were more important and more enduring. The first of these was a belief in the nation as a natural political community, as alluded to previously. Le Pen's definition of politics illustrates this: "Politics is a science, the most important of all human sciences, that of the common interest of the people and of the nation. Political parties are not at liberty to do with it as they wish. But politics is also a calling, that of service to the community, in the form of disinterested devotion to the cause of natural entities: Family, City, and above all, Nation."[8] The yearly worship of Joan of Arc (a pre-revolutionary heroine) fits neatly into this.

---

8. Jean-Marie Le Pen, "J'appelle la France à combattre le déclin, la décadence et la servitude", *National Hebdo*, 12 November 1987.

No explanation needed

Underpinning the vision of this order is not just hierarchy but instinctively shared values. And the function of values here is that they serve as silent guides. Because they are of a shared past, they belong to everyone. And because they belong to everyone, they need no explanation. They are the secret code of the nation, one that cannot easily be adopted by outsiders. In fact, they are useful to tell the outsiders from the insiders: "You're one of us if all of this seems obvious". The "true person", the "true patriot" is detectable by their capacity to live by the codes of the nation because it is obvious to them. And it is obvious to them, because it is a natural part of who they are.

Absent democracy

Conspicuously absent from this construct is an allegiance to democracy. Both the Republic and democracy were still rejected in the FN's foundational appeal. And the ballot box was adopted for strategic purposes only: it was simply a better tool in order to be a player in de Gaulle's Fifth Republic. But, even a reconceived and self-serving form of democracy, was not part of the FN's conceptual ideals early in the FN's trajectory. In this respect the early FN is only a prototype: it still owes more to the far right of the earlier part of the twentieth century, to basic nationalism, and to some extent to a version of conservatism than to populism. What sets it apart from the far right at that point is Le Pen's vision of the practice of politics and an emerging, and quite radically different, understanding of the relationship between voters and politicians.

Prototyping a new political relationship

For Le Pen, despite a display of acceptance for the rules of the democratic game, the name of the game was actually subversion. Whilst the founding of the party was all about renouncing far-right violence and embracing a more acceptable profile for electoral purposes (what many have referred to as the strategy of "de-demonization" – essentially, the pursuit of respectability)[9], there remained both the man's natural ten-

---

9. Gombin points out in his book on Marine Le Pen that the aim was not to "tone down" the ideas to make them more mainstream, but rather to create a broad

dency toward provocation, as well as a desire (and a real plan) to subvert the codes of the Republic as often as he could. This might be through references to the monarchy, controversial statements about the Third Reich; or simply the refusal to condemn the street-fighting that inevitably accompanied the FN's early rallies (during which the FN security detail regularly beat up any adversaries) and all this through the codes of the Republic, in order to undermine it from within. The point here is that Le Pen was always in a number of ways challenging the legitimacy of law and order. The remedy to the decline of France might have to be administered initially through a conversion to the ballot box, but the belief in the necessary and potentially violent eradication of what Le Pen saw as the rot inside the French system, was never too far below the surface. The pronouncements and gaffes all fit neatly into both the kind of "dog-whistle" politics that characterize movements that flirt with extremism, but also with the ideas discussed in the previous section: the spontaneity that goes with the natural order, the common sense that underpins the values of the people, and the vocation to act as the mouthpiece of those who have been rendered voiceless by a corrupt elite.

"I am merely saying ..."

Le Pen is one of the earliest characters to adopt populism's key trope, namely a claim to "being real". In this respect Le Pen's pronouncements serve several functions. Initially, the obvious one was simply to attract attention at a time when the media was not paying any attention to the FN and where Le Pen spent a great deal of time complaining of his unfair marginalization by the mainstream media. When he was finally handed the microphone, he made the most of it and generated interest for days. A classic case, at the time, of "no such thing as bad publicity". But mainly, the "gaffes" were part theatre for supporters and part provocation for the establishment. As theatre they were the bona fide display of his good faith: that he was who he said he was, that he was one of the people, and he thought like them. And, in many respects, whether or not this was true, he gave them permission to think and to speak as he did. As he often said himself, "I am merely saying what everyone else is

---

enough church to accommodate both radicals and moderates (Gombin 2016: 145).

thinking". The subtext being that he would not be bullied into the norms of the establishment.

So, many of Le Pen's choice phrases were aimed at the activists and delivered in large party meetings. It is on such occasions that he made statements about racial inequality (in 1996), or the play on words around a government minister's name and gas chambers (in 1988 at the end of the FN Party conference), or on the doubts he harboured about the French football team and the fact that given its multicultural composition he was not sure they would be able to sing the Marseillaise (also 1996).

But the "gaffes" – which, as I've said, were very rarely "gaffes", but mostly calculated provocations – were also about provoking a reaction in the well-meaning liberal elite. This was useful in terms of showing that he was not going to be cowed by their codes. But it also demonstrated that he was willing to put his mouth where his guts were and willing to take risks on behalf of the people. That he was different from the other politicians, because he was willing to be himself even if it went against the status quo. As he himself declared, "Today the general consensus deprives citizens of necessary political competition. We are not prisoners of that consensus, and therefore retain the freedom to speak our truth. I have done that, I will continue to do that. I call a spade a spade, and the Socialists scoundrels".[10] Bear in mind, that this was 25 years before Trump and Salvini, and nearly 15 years before Beppe Grillo of the Five Star Movement burst onto the political scene. It was trail-blazing.

Nowhere was this more visible than around the legacy of the Second World War.[11] Le Pen's tactic was not undiluted revisionism, but a propensity to call some facts into question, and to suggest that there is a hierarchy of offences that each person can evaluate as they see fit – a refusal in other words, to go along with mainstream statements on human rights or crimes against humanity. Le Pen's referring to the gas chambers as a "historical detail" of the Second World War is a case in

---

10. Jean-Marie Le Pen, *Le Monde*, 21 January 1992.
11. It is worth keeping in mind that the 1990s were a particularly fraught time in France when it came to questions about the Second Word War: some of the most high-profile prosecutions against known-Nazi collaborators (Barbier in 1987, Touvier in 1994 and Papon in 1998) hit the headlines, as well as accusations against then President, François Mitterrand for his role in the Pétain regime.

point (I'm not saying they did not exist, I'm saying I never saw one ... some historians legitimately debate this question, etc).[12]

For decades there was a real debate as to whether the provocative statements and the offensive phrases undermined the whole enterprise of respectability set in motion by Le Pen, but the fact is that they established what was to become a characteristic of European populism: the reliance on provocation to create the impression of authenticity, of having – contrary to all other politicians who are accused of mincing their words and, later, of political correctness – nothing to hide.

Lies, and more lies

The lies fit into this great scheme of subversion and disruption. Both the direct – let's call it "inter-personal" – lying (directly to the interlocutor), as well as the grand lying that took the form of dissimulation, barely disguised fraud, or the assertion of known falsehoods. Jean-Marie Le Pen certainly is not the first politician to lie; however, what he does – and what populists in general do – is use the lie not as a cover up, but as an instrument of subversion. This is the difference between not wanting to be caught lying, and lying for the purposes of sending a signal, namely to demonstrate a willingness to do anything to advance the cause of one's people, or to signal that one is entirely above the establishment's conventions, or even to show one's flawed humanity and a relaxed attitude toward these natural, human failings. Lying as a demonstration of one's irrepressibly authentic nature: what could be more sincere than that?

Getting into their heads

For Jean-Marie Le Pen, as for populists who followed, the claim to authenticity went further and took the form of directness. Beyond the capacity to act as the mouthpiece of the people, the other aspect that the FN privileged from very early on was direct, quasi-personal, contact. Many observers have pointed to the quite traditional quality of the great FN gatherings; that for all the party's hatred of the communists, the

---

12. Jean-Marie Le Pen, *Le Grand Jury RTL*, 13 September 1987.

_ _vents very closely resembled mass Soviet rallies characterized by the presence of the great leader and his interminable speeches. Anyone who had ever attended one of the FN's great gatherings knew what to expect: a triumphal welcome complete with red, white and blue lights and enormous stage, the Marseillaise blaring, followed by several hours of haranguing by the great man. On several occasions people around me fell asleep. Gombin notes in his book that for all the talk of the charisma of the leader, this did not exactly come naturally (Gombin 2016: chapter 2). It took many years, a highly centralized party, no obvious rivals (or at least, none that were allowed to emerge) and the imposition of his personality at every possible opportunity, for his leadership to be unequivocally recognized.

But aside from his ideas, Le Pen recognized the value of new forms of communication. Long before the World Wide Web, Le Pen used France's precursor to the internet, the national Minitel system (an online interactive Videotex system accessible through telephone lines) to connect the membership to the party through 3615FN and 3615LePen (the FN's Minitel addresses). The Minitel is largely regarded as a symbol of France's die-hard belief in its technological uniqueness, often at the expense of scaling-up or of commercial viability. But Minitel was an early foray into the sort of connectivity that the Web would subsequently bring: by 1991, over 5 million terminals were in use. It was free of charge, and state sponsored (in fact some argue that it was so good that it put France a full five years behind the rest of the world when the Web finally hit) (Mailland 2017). It connected millions of households to information for free and Le Pen was the first one to avail himself of that connection in the mid-1980s. It stood to reason that the FN was also the first French political party to have a website (in 1994), and even the first, in 2006, to have a virtual office on *Second Life*, the online virtual world. In one conversation in 1997 Le Pen was quite clear, and long before others:

> I'm not sure how these things really work, but I know that for us whether it is the Minitel or the web, it is not just about giving information, it is about building a new relationship with our voters. These people are impatient, they are starting to realize that everything could be happening a lot faster than it is and that politicians are just sitting around. And so that's what we're giving them. You dial us (or log in? or ... anyways, you connect

to us) and 'zap' we're in your head, we know what you want, we know why you want it. And you can just … ask. That's what we've been about for 25 years: getting people to really ask for what they think they deserve. But now we can even ask them directly – all of them. Our database is huge.[13]

As analysts of the FN many of us have spent a great deal of time counting ideological angels on a pin head. Was this truly a far-right discourse? How much of this was revolutionary rather than conservative? Was Le Pen a new form of far right (shaped by the "new right")? Or was he simply a dinosaur? One of the questions we dwelt on for far too long was why so many people wanted to "go back" to options that had been discredited in the early part of the century, or put another way, why was the far right resurgent? The question was a valid one, as there is an obvious far-right legacy at the heart of the FN/RN. But the interesting point was the fact that Jean-Marie Le Pen was busy creating something new; tapping into new political aspirations. Far from being old wine in new bottles, under Le Pen, FN had more akin to new wine in old bottles. He – and his daughter Marine – saw the advantages of social media early on. But much more to the point, he detected a change in the electorate: new aspirations and new appetites that would work in the party's favour (by fanning the flames of impatience vis-à-vis existing mainstream parties). The story of Marine Le Pen is therefore both one of adaptation and one of continuing to pursue subversive politics.

From Front national to Rassemblement national: transformation with Marine?

I first met Marine Le Pen by accident. I was visiting her father in Montretout when she burst into his study: "Papa", she said, "I've found the interview of the guy who says you carved up his leg during the Algerian war. I've got it downstairs on tape". We followed her to the television room where a paused tape awaited us. She switched it on. An elderly Algerian began his testimonial to an interviewer: "Of course, I recognize him", he said, "it was him [J-MLP] who did this to me. You

---

13. Jean-Marie Le Pen, conversation in Montretout, 10 September 1997.

think I'd forget the face of a man who did this?" He pointed to his calf, a good portion of which had been carved out and bore a deep, ugly scar. Jean-Marie and his daughter burst out laughing. It wasn't a monstrous laugh, of horror film magnitude, but a dismissive "what can you do?" kind of laugh, which sort of made it worse. The cruelty didn't register. And my presence certainly didn't stop them, although I can't say I was particularly heroic in my protestations: I was frozen. "Can you believe the gall?" said Marine. "What an idiot, I should have done much worse to him", replied her dad.

Despite my deep unease at the scene, I have since been grateful to have been an unwitting witness to it. Everything I have ever needed to know about Marine Le Pen was contained in that first ten-minute encounter: her strange and ambivalent relationship to her father (after all she was essentially doing the job of a zealous intern, but with the allegiance of a daughter); the strange mix of excitability ("you have to come see this NOW") and calm (little reaction to a sight that might have knocked others sideways, as it did me); and that bizarre double-allegiance to him and to the party – who was she working for as she sat through tape after tape looking for the interview? In many respects, until she finally marginalized him out of the party in 2015, Marine Le Pen's life has been about balancing his party, his acts, and her vision.

Marine's first official FN appearance took place on 5 May 2002, at the party celebrating her father's, then, historic result, and his reaching the second round of the presidential election (against Jacques Chirac). In the parliamentary elections held a month later, Marine ran for a seat in Lens (a working-class, socialist bastion on the outskirts of Lille) and she too made it to the run-off with a result of 24.2 per cent. At the time, her father was fond of repeating "the apple never falls far from the tree". And there is the whole question: how far did she need to fall, in order to be even more effective than her father?

The balancing act: past and future

Marine's role in the party was often thought to be about ensuring continuity, not just in terms of filiation, but also because she sided with her father when the party divided between her father and Bruno Mégret in 1998 (unlike her sister Marie Caroline, who had been far more involved than her in the party to begin with, but chose to leave). In that respect she was held to be the continuation of the traditional FN. This is something of a paradox, because she was probably ideologically closer to Mégret who was much more disposed toward alliances with the rest of the right, and above all much more committed to turning the party into an effective electoral machine, rather than maintain its rawer, "movement" qualities, which perpetuated the impression of a disruptive political force, rather than a credible, electable political party.

But from 2002 Marine was essentially in charge of making the most (or at least handling as best she could) the generational renewal in the FN electorate. The membership had already become substantially different: these were now people who had joined the party in the 1990s, and for whom it was an already established political party. There was no question of subjecting them to the remnants of some of the foundational dysfunctions or hesitations that had initially plagued the party and were still to some extent visible in J.-M. Le Pen and some of his close allies. So, in 2002, Marine Le Pen founded, "Génération Le Pen", a movement within the party designed to appeal to these younger members, or at least to this new wave of voters and members.

On her father's retirement in 2012, Marine was elected president of the FN with two third of the members' votes, beating FN stalwart Bruno Gollnisch. Both were seen as faithful to Jean-Marie's doctrine, but Marine was the much younger of the two and her selection by the membership was a clear sign that they felt new blood was needed at the helm. The FN's share of the vote was down (10.4% in the first round of the presidential election of 2007 won by Sarkozy who effectively trounced the FN with his own patriotic message), and the membership looked to Marine to revive the fortunes of the party. This, on the surface of it, is the story of the party under Marine. In charge of renewal, but forever caught between her father's legacy (and a personalized movement) or the option to professionalize the party (as Mégret had tried to do).[14]

---

14. All parties tend to go through a version of this, and populist parties more so than others. At the core of populism is a rejection of traditional professional politics, but elections mean they need to buy into this process to be effective; in doing so, they lose part of what made them appealing to certain voters to begin with. In the case of Marine Le Pen there is a nice oedipal twist to the whole story (and, at last, the inevitable public row with her father in 2015, when she decisively distanced the party from many of his more outrageous comments and, finally, expelled him).

And the ideological split got worse: as the FN attempted to broaden its appeal, it had to maintain both a more liberal economic line (to match the preferences of its original, petty-bourgeois, small-business owners, voters in the south of France) as well as a more statist, welfarist, interventionist stance (designed to cater to the growing, more modest working-class electorate that they were pursuing in northern France). The tension was two-fold: there was a genuine hesitation as to which economic model to choose; plus the risk of alienating one or the other electorate if both messages were used in tandem. In the end, the FN chose (although perhaps not emphatically enough) what Sarah de Lange has identified as the new winning formula – a kind of pro-welfare, protectionist national interventionism – having calculated that the working-class reservoir of voters was perhaps larger, and more likely to have nowhere else to go (de Lange 2007).

But by the 2017 presidential election, Marine Le Pen was still hesitating. The result was Dad's party minus the overt racism plus the welfare state. And complete ambiguity on the euro. Her campaign video is a perfect illustration of the difficult balancing act she attempted: "I am a woman", she says, "I am a mother", "I am a lawyer". But the background is classic Le Pen Senior: the coastline of Brittany, Marine at the helm of a sailboat. More than a nod in the direction of her father's many electoral posters on which he sported classic sailing gear, or was photographed against the background of a Breton lighthouse, or crashing waves. She ends with: "Yes, I want to re-establish order in France".[15] The combination of soft-focus sailing pictures, authoritative-looking official visits, and a string of patriotic repetitions ("I am passionately French, endurably French, intensely French") – all of it designed to highlight this new, rare combination of womanhood, strength, passion and expertise – falls entirely flat.

Le Pen paid a high price for this: while her score in the 2017 election was respectable (21.3% in the first round, which allowed her to go through to the second round, which saw her reach 33.3% of the vote and defeat by Emmanuel Macron), her performance left the party wondering whether she had it in her to lead them to victory. That 25–30 per

---

15. "*Mettre de l'ordre*" is the expression she uses: somewhere between "tidy up" and "re-establish order".

cent bar around which the party has been hovering since 2014, seemed impossible to get over, but more to the point, the contest showed her fraying at the edges when faced with some key issues, including her attitude toward the EU, and specifically the FN's views on whether or not to advocate France's withdrawal from the euro. By and large, the dilemma is at the heart of the FN: the choice between a protectionist nationalist view for the new working-class electorate, and the more liberal (pro-EU view) of an older bourgeois electorate who feared for its savings and its pensions should France attempt to leave the euro. That fundamental question regarding the FN's economic position is still unresolved and has cost it dearly, there is no doubt. Especially given the way she handled it in a crucial final television debate with Macron, during which the combination of her confusion and her stridency sealed her fate against Macron's technocratic poise.

Beneath the surface: the final populist adaptation

The year 2017 marks a significant turning point for the party. By the end of the endless French electoral cycle (party primaries, two rounds of presidential elections and two rounds of parliamentary elections), Marine's position in the party appeared tenuous. She had performed badly at a crucial moment against Macron, and the party had gained far fewer MPs than they had promised their supporters (only eight). Many wondered if her days were not numbered and wondered also whether the party would recover from the disappointment that the over-promising had generated in its base.

But a couple of things are worth mentioning. The first is that Marine's attitude and behaviour after the elections placed her in that great tradition of defeat and recovery: she disappeared for a time, while clinging to power, changed the party's name from the rather bellicose Front National to the more welcoming Rassemblement National (one further step away from the far right, and one step closer to the mainstream right's former party name under Chirac from 1976 to 2002, Rassemblement pour la République (Rally for the Republic). But she has also made a convincing bid for much younger voters and taken full advantage of social media and the kinds of messages she and the party can best communicate through it.

Second, these elections – and perhaps because her position was indeed in jeopardy – allowed her in the end to emerge as the uncontested leader. Partly because Marine has been very careful to groom no one as her successor, she is, for now, the party's only hope. But also, because there is in her routine attitude to the swings and roundabouts of politics something of the indefatigable warrior. But also, in her willingness to accept her defeat, something of that commitment to being herself; in some respects she is, to voters, a more authentic character than her father, because they have witnessed her transformation into who she is today. In the context of a populist party, that particular type of authenticity, is a very powerful political weapon: she has evolved in full view, has both won and been defeated in full view. To her voters, she has nothing to hide.

Marine and her voters

As early as 2002 Marine Le Pen set about renewing both the voting base – in age, gender and class – and the party's personnel. But it is in 2011, that she took the biggest turn. Ideologically, as Dézé (2015) points out, Marine Le Pen made very few changes to the party's main appeals (the people, the betrayal of the people, the disconnection of an illegitimate elite), though she has added a major emphasis on democracy, but what she did do was change the way the party interacted with its voters, which meant framing her relationships differently, putting forward new people to interact with the fragmented base of the party, and growing the number of channels and ways of reaching out.

On the RN website and in her speeches, the usual themes have pride of place: Europe turning France into a vassal state; plenty of references to the "sacred duty of the French soldier in protecting his sacred land" (and the First World War "warriors" fallen for freedom); "millenarian villages"; "swindled farmers who are guardians of France's sacred earth", etc, with a liberal sprinkling of misquotes, lies and threats. But above all, what now dominates is the constant reference to proximity, directness and immediate access. As I write, a few months ahead of the 2019 European Parliament elections and as the "Gilets Jaunes" continue to gather in various French towns, Le Pen offers the following: "My project is a proximity revolution. Democratic proximity: I want citizens to control political decision-making directly; [...] Economic proximity:

[…] no French person, wherever they are, must ever be forgotten".[16] In terms of discourse Marine adopted early on the themes of closeness, but since the presidential election of 2017 (and in part, no doubt, as a reaction to Emmanuel Macron's repeated references to his Jupiterian presidency), she has made "proximity" and "connection" the main theme of her political programme.

In organizational terms Marine Le Pen turned her attention to what she referred to as "the digital imperative" immediately upon her election to the head of the party in 2011. Having been a trail-blazer back in 2002, in 2011 she set up a new special unit within the movement, the National Secretariat for Digital Communications (SNCN) headed initially by two national secretaries at the time, Julien Sanchez and David Rachline. Rachline, who had been particularly close to Marine (and been leader of the FN's youth movement that she created) went on to lead the FN/RN's digital strategy, and Sanchez has been the party's spokesperson since 2017. Aside from Emmanuel Macron's official presidential Facebook page (2.3 million followers), Le Pen's Facebook page is by far the most popular on the French political landscape (with 1.5 million followers). The "digital unit" is now 15 people strong.

Digital as the main strategy

By the French presidential election of 2017, Marine Le Pen (and Jean Luc Mélenchon) were way ahead of their opponents in terms of digital outreach and mobilization. As she launched her presidential campaign in Lyon on 4 February 2017, Marine Le Pen exhorted the audience to turn to social media, both to spread the word, but also to have access to her "unfiltered by the gatekeepers of the traditional media" (who the FN/RN has always accused of treating them unfairly either by ignoring the party, or by covering it in disparaging terms). "We want to break with the norms of traditional politics" she said, before introducing a person who was going to, over the next few hours, give her troops all the digital training and advice they needed. Aside from her own accounts Marine is also known to maintain a few pseudonym accounts, where she allows her avatar to be far more radical in her criticism of her rivals

16. Rassemblement national, https://rassemblementnational.fr/le-projet-de-marine-le-pen/ (accessed 12 March 2019).

and enemies. As for the party itself, aside from its following on social media, it benefits from close networks with all sorts of more radical political and conspiracy sites known as the "fachosphere" (referred to in RN circles as the "patriot-sphere": websites that range from the crudely anti-Semitic, to the madly conspiratorial).[17]

Julien Boyadjian (2015) points to three ways in which the party has benefited from the Web: first, he argues, a social media and web presence allows you to make the most of giant numbers. In the case of the RN (and the FN since the 2012 presidential campaign) the various RN websites exhort the visitor to "sign up and sign up your friends" and "help us reach another 500,000 of fans" so we can "make Marine the biggest political personality on the web". It creates pathways for visitors to give themselves daily missions and daily targets of documents and links to share as widely as possible: "Let's act together and make sure that our ideas and our policies reach as many people as possible. We've compiled a list of missions the success of which depends on every one of you! To help us increase our audience, help us every day by accomplishing your missions! For every mission you will earn points! Together let's help everyone discover our proposals for our country!"[18] Secondly, the various FN official sites can act as a "respectability" prism; in other words, the party can resort to all the trappings of a respectable, mainstream party. And thirdly, the Web, aside from everything else, allows the party to have its cake and eat it: to appear mainstream on its own platforms whilst allowing others to radicalize their message on their platforms without the RN getting its hands dirty.

What's next for the RN?

So where does the "doyen" of right-wing populist parties in Europe go from here? That role of "doyenne" is in part the role that Marine seeks

---

17. The websites www.fdesouche.com and https://ripostelaique.com/ are amongst the most influential. Anti-Semitic, anti-pluralist and anti-immigrant, these sites enable the RN to spread its message far and wide without having to come directly into contact with them. On the broader theme of the FN/RN's networks, see Mestre & Monot 2015.

18. See https://www.lespatriotes.net/pages/comment-gagner-des-points.html (cited in Boyadjian 2015: 158).

to play, both in France and at the European level. While she is pipped at the post by someone like Salvini in terms of electoral success and access to political power, she plays a different role on the European scene. Perceived as less mercurial than Salvini or Orban, in part because she draws her authenticity from that long reinvention of herself in the public eye (in France and abroad), she remains in many ways an ideological and organizational reference point on the European scene: the FN was, after all, the first of these parties to access the institutions of the EU. And with her MEPs she is set to wield substantial power. That is not to say that she is not focused on the French landscape, but the EU has always been one of the party's most effective stages and this is set to continue. Indeed, she may well become more powerful there than in France.

In addition, what could have been an insuperable obstacle – the cultivation of her mainstream persona whilst continuing to be disruptive and anti-systemic, and at the same time remaining authentic in both personal and party terms (a tall order) – was resolved through her embracing of both a semi-traditional French political persona, in combination with a dose of straight-speaking (her father's brand), and the party's digital presence that is largely separate from her persona. She has a personal account and she uses it regularly but does not use it to engage casually. She has learnt to inhabit these various spheres simultaneously. It means that her brand of authenticity is particular (less bombastic, more discreet), but just as effective given the FN baggage.

Finally, the RN is an extremely successful challenger party. It has written the handbook on populist politics in Europe and paved the way for others by bringing a new form of authentic politics to the very heart of politics, just as this became the name of the game through social media. But more to the point, Marine Le Pen and the RN are, as I write, the main opposition to President Macron. And even though its local implantation is weak, and it is doing well in the context of very low electoral mobilization (Dézé 2015), and a party system in disarray, it is at the moment the main party of opposition in France. But there is also a more interesting way in which the RN is a challenger party, and potentially reinventing the manner in which populist parties work. Some light can be shed on this by looking at the Gilets Jaunes crisis. Almost as soon as the Gilets Jaunes emerged in mid-November 2018, data tended to show that whilst most of the protesters were non-voters, a significant portion of them declared a sympathy for Marine Le Pen's party. What followed was revealing both in terms of the Gilets Jaunes and the RN. The Gilets Jaunes are a fascinating instance of mobilization because, while many labelled them populist, they seemed more like an instance of agitation propaganda. But these are no longer incompatible: they were claiming to speak in the name of the people, and demanding a different kind of more direct and transparent democracy; and they certainly seemed to be prone to conspiracy theories. Despite the diversity of their demands, and the fact that they brought together protesters who claimed a proximity both to the right and to the left, it is difficult to dismiss them as *not* an instance of populist mobilization. And their refusal – or their struggle – to designate or elect leaders does not detract from that. They were in many respects the height of authentic spontaneity, to the extent that to begin with they seemed to surprise even themselves. So it is worth thinking about what such movements tell us about how populism is likely to evolve. In the context of fragmented political systems and availability of social media, it is not far-fetched to think that not only are populist politics going to be an important and permanent feature of our political landscapes, but also that populist parties as we know them will become more and more able to loosely connect with movements such as the Gilets Jaunes and their successors. Marine Le Pen's attitude was a case in point: even though she stood to lose a few points if the Gilets Jaunes ran their own European lists, she nevertheless was careful to quietly support them. Unlike Jean-Luc Mélenchon who made overtures that were rebuked by the protesters, Le Pen's pronouncements were just supportive enough, without being invasive. Instead she let her parallel social media sphere do the work and seemed happy to include their stances in her broad populist church. The RN may be giving us a glimpse of what the populist galaxy will look like in the not so distant future.

Challengers to Marine Le Pen exist both on her right and on her left. On her right she is up against the growing popularity of her niece Marion Maréchal-Le Pen (who, tellingly, dropped the "Le Pen" name in 2018);[19] And on her left she is confronted with the populism of Jean-Luc

---

19. Maréchal-Le Pen joined the party in 2008 at the age of 18 and later became MP for the département of Vaucluse in the 2012 legislative elections. At 22, she was France's youngest ever deputy, and the FN's first representative in the National Assembly since 1997. More economically liberal than the FN leadership, more strident, Maréchal is disinclined toward the party's new welfarism. She is also far more socially conservative on issues such as same-sex marriage, and abortion.

Mélenchon – less numerically and electorally successful than her own, but capable of delivering a blisteringly personal and direct message.

Enter stage left: La France Insoumise

The only time I met Jean-Luc Mélenchon – in the run up to the 2017 presidential and legislative elections – he called on me to ask him a question, then told me to "shut up" and then barked at me to stop interrupting him, ending his sentence with a rather cutting "who the hell do you think you are?" A reassuring "there-there" tap on my shoulder from the stranger sitting behind me suggested that others had walked a mile in my shoes. That brush with the great man sums up his political career rather well: Jean Luc Mélenchon is quite good at getting people to come into a room to listen to him; but less sure what to do with them once they are there (which certainly does not include listening to them).

In its rigidity and categorical tone, Mélenchon's personal blog gives the impression that he is both extremely talented, and his own worst enemy. Entitled "The era of the people", the blog comes across as part maniacal hit-list, part sycophantic roll of honour: Turkey, Marine Le Pen, Macron, the Fifth Republic, the media, the PM, and the United States all get black marks and condemnation. But when I visited, the Gilets Jaunes (who Mélenchon had been wooing for weeks) were getting lots of stars and ticks. And yet, they want nothing to do with him. A paradox given that polls suggest that many yellow vests felt politically close to his party, yet none wanted him at any of their demonstrations. And neither do French trade unions, to whom he has sent rather mixed messages. In other words, many on the more radical fringes of the French left want nothing to do with the leader of France's more radical left populist party. And his self-presentation as doctrinaire and unbending does not help.

She overtly defines herself as the "ideological heir" to her grandfather Jean-Marie Le Pen. Finally, Where Marine had tried to downplay the FN's attitudes toward Islam, Marion unflinchingly declared that "France is not a home for Islam; If some French people want to practice as Muslims, this has to be on the condition that they respect our way of life, one that has been influenced by Greece and Rome and that has been fashioned by 16 centuries of Christianity".

To some extent, Mélenchon's political career is a reflection of where he finds himself today: everyone recognizes that he is a gifted speaker, and a cultured man, but nobody trusts him. This relative failure is of particular relevance to us, because it forces the issue of trust and the status of lies and authenticity in the populist imagination. Why has Mélenchon not been more successful? He has mastered both the themes and the instruments of populism, in many ways better than Marine Le Pen; his party is more recent, but he came fourth in the presidential election of 2017 with a non-negligible share of the vote (19.58%), and within a hair's breadth of Marine Le Pen (21.30%) and Francois Fillon (20.01%). And why is success certain to elude him further?

A party borne of a fight against the EU

Mélenchon's political career began in the 1970s when he joined the Parti socialiste (PS) and went on to serve as a municipal councillor (1983), general councillor (1985) and later senator (1986) for the PS. A Trotskyite in his youth, whilst at the PS Mélenchon adopted a more moderate approach to politics. Between 2000 and 2002, he was a junior minister for vocational education in Lionel Jospin's Gauche Plurielle coalition government. But he was always on the left of the PS, and frequently found himself at odds with his colleagues.

The tensions became unsustainable after France's referendum on the ratification of the EU constitution in 2005. He campaigned for the socialist "No" vote, going against the majority in the party. He left in 2008 and formed the Parti de gauche (PG) in 2009. The PG was in an alliance of left-wing movements known as the Front de gauche (FG), a grouping formed to contest the 2009 European elections. It was also the platform that Mélenchon used to launch his first bid for the presidency in 2012. Whilst there was broad ideological overlap across the movements in the FG, the foremost catalyst for the formation of the alliance was a collective opposition to the EU as a neoliberal economic project driven by an elite hell-bent on suppressing wage growth at the expense of the working class (Escalona & Vieira 2014). (For anyone familiar with the UK, this sounds a lot like Jeremy Corbyn's position on the EU).

Standing out in policy terms

The anti-establishment mantra is at the heart of Mélenchon's rhetoric and of his programme. He has been a longstanding advocate for a sixth Republic and during his presidential campaign, he told a Paris crowd that he wished to "lead a citizen insurrection" against the "Republican monarchy". Calls for a new regime were formulated in classic populist *dégagisme* (a "drain the swamp" kind of appeal): "Just get out so that we can finally abolish the privileges of finance, and above all of all those who are a part of the insolent cast that has usurped every power and shared it amongst its members".[20] His programme centred on a "constituent assembly" that would draw up a new constitution that would then be approved by referendum. Direct democracy, referendums by popular initiative, and a system that would allow all citizens to propose their own laws were the icing on Mélenchon's populist cake.

... and in rhetorical terms

Above everything else that the French seem to recognize about Mélenchon is a particular mix of erudition and brutality: he can famously quote poets, philosophers and economists; he has referred to himself as someone who "raises consciousness and provokes debate" (a combination of Jean-Paul Sartre and *The Matrix*'s "red pill"), but he would never use the political term "woke" because it is grammatically incorrect. But alongside the intellectual references (that are more than window dressing, he is a well-read man) Mélenchon delights in courting controversy: he has referred to Trump as a "*crétin borné*" (a thicko), to the new education minister as "*tordu*" (a bit of a freak), and labelled some of President Macron's followers of as "*une meute*", "*une horde*" and "*un ramassis*" (a pack, a hoard, and a "sorry bunch") (Tremblay 2017). These views, widely reported in the media, contribute to his image as a *franc-parleur* (a straight-talker). Add to this some striking sartorial

20. *Le Monde*, 'Mélenchon souhaite la VIe République pour "une société dans laquelle on veut vivre"' 18 March 2017; available at: https://www.lemonde.fr/election-presidentielle-2017/article/2017/03/18/melenchon-souhaite-la-vie-republique-pour-une-societe-dans-laquelle-on-veut-vivre_5096904_4854003.html (accessed 19 September 2018).

choices – throughout the 2017 campaign, and particularly during the debates, he chose to wear a very distinctive jacket without lapels, à la Mao Zedong, that gave him the appearance of a bold "man of the people cum peasant" – and Mélenchon clinched his position as a character on the political scene but not necessarily as a politician.[21]

The relationship with voters

La France Insoumise (FI) has never sought the party label. In fact it has consistently claimed to want to function as a "decentralized network". At its inception the movement focused on the creation of an online participatory platform (not a million miles from that created a few years earlier by Beppe Grillo for his Five Star Movement). The platform was designed to aggregate ideas and organize online debates. But originally, the real objective was to follow-up by implementing the results of online discussion at the local level. Some of it worked: the platform essentially allowed for the crowdsourcing of FI's electoral manifestos (see Hamburger 2018). The similarities here, and elsewhere in terms of tactics, with Beppe Grillo's Five Star Movement (which I'll discuss in the next chapter) are striking.

Again, like Five Stars, when it was launched in February 2016, FI cast itself in the role of the outsider and as a new kind of movement (the party bit came distinctly second). Its main purpose, it argued, was to challenge mainstream politics through a different kind of political action. FI made it a point to select ordinary people as its candidates. Much like Emmanuel Macron, the movement was obsessed with "civil society"; but whereas Macron recruited entrepreneurs and intellectuals, FI went for call-centre operators, librarians, and nursing assistants (*ibid.*: 102–103).

---

21. He and members of the parliamentary FI party also took a stand in the National Assembly by refusing to wear ties, evoking France's revolutionary tradition to portray it as an expression of popular will: "*Il y avait des sans-culottes, il y aura maintenant des sans-cravates*"; see L. Boichot, "Jean-Luc Mélenchon refuse symboliquement de porter la cravate à l'Assemblée", *Le Figaro*, 27 June 2017. Available at: http://www.lefigaro.fr/politique/2017/06/27/01002-20170627ART FIG00282-jean-luc-melenchon-refuse-symboliquement-de-porter-la-cravate-a -l-assemblee.php (accessed 20 September 2018).

As pointed out by Hamburger, their inspiration was an unlikely American source: the community organizer Saul Alinsky: "Like Alinsky once did in Chicago's slums, FI launched a series of door-to-door listening campaigns in the low-income *banlieues* of France's major cities [...] by going directly to the country's most disaffected citizens, FI could not only learn which issues matter to people, but also establish a human connection with people who might otherwise be wary of left-wing organizers" (*ibid.*: 109). This was the movement's way of connecting with and mobilizing ordinary people so that they might feel confident enough to take on elites. As reported by Hamburger, "Chaibi asserted that LFI's well-publicized clashes with representatives of the status quo also fit into Alinsky's playbook. LFI is convinced that through such actions, it can sustain a vibrant movement culture". For our purposes here, this is interesting again because it points to similarities with Five Stars and Grillo, but also because disruption and the authenticity of the people are seen to go hand in hand. The contrast between the "movement culture" evoked by FI and the aims of Marine Le Pen's RN are worth noting because it illustrates why, despite similarities that make them both populist, populists on the right and on the left differ fundamentally in their notion of the people. The FN, and the RN has never sought (or even claimed) to give people a voice through mobilization – the claim was that they might be heard by the leader and they should make their will known through the ballot box. However much Mélenchon's authoritarian personality belies his capacity to delegate anything to anyone, FI's founding logic is one in which the people are not an organic mass, but rather a collection of citizens choosing to work together.

As for Mélenchon's digital strategy, it is, much as for the RN, the heart of the matter. Having famously labelled himself "the candidate of the geeks" and held two simultaneous campaign meetings by projecting himself as a hologram, Mélenchon was hell-bent on cornering the digital campaign market. He has his own personal blog, his personal (crowdfunded) independent media channel *Le Média* as well, of course, as a personal Facebook page (on which he has one million followers), a popular YouTube channel, and even a game "Fiscal Kombat" (a reference to video game *Mortal Kombat*) starring Jean-Luc Mélenchon as a great wealth redistributor.

But above all, Mélenchon has famously relied on a rather ruthless army of supporters and internet trolls as well as extremely centralized messaging and hard discipline inside the party. As the *Canard Enchaîné*, France's best-informed source of political gossip, reported in April, a petition for more internal democracy within FI was rejected by former Mélenchon campaign spokesman Manuel Bompard (*ibid.*: 109–10). Mélenchon himself famously declared that he did not want FI "to be democratic, he wanted it to be collective". And during the election in 2017, a host of well documented stories surfaced regarding the coordinated bullying by the Mélenchon campaign and his supporters of any critical voice.

Nul points for authenticity

Mélenchon is a fascinating case study of a populist that can "talk the talk" but cannot quite "walk the walk". Yet walking that walk is precisely what populism requires. Mélenchon and his party have entirely understood the role that directness and authenticity play in contemporary populism; they have completely understood that authenticity is the magic ingredient. And while his lieutenants can pull it off (François Ruffin is a case in point of someone whose demeanour, rhetoric and countenance vis-à-vis supporters and detractors is one of consistent confidence), the leader himself has more trouble.

The trouble with Jean-Luc is that he is a man of performance: for him, the role of FI leader is what the French would call "*un rôle de composition*": a complex, multifaceted role. And this is where trouble begins, because authenticity cannot be performed. Sincerity and honesty can be, but authenticity cannot. And however gifted an actor Mélenchon, sometimes the mask slips. Because there is a mask. However odious Trump or Berlusconi might be, what you see is what you get. It is not what is revealed that is problematic, but the fact that there is something to be revealed. When in October 2018 Mélenchon lost his temper and filmed the police raid in his office, whilst barking that they could not enter because they would be violating the Republic and he "was the Republic"; or when, incensed and disappointed at his fourth place in 2017, he failed to come out and rally for Macron (at least not right away), thereby suggesting that his loss was more important than protecting the Republic, even from Marine Le Pen, whom he clearly and genuinely loathes; or when, caught off guard he humiliated a journalist by imitating her country accent in front of live media. In all of these instances, he might have recovered from the sin – after all Trump and Berlusconi and Jean-Marie Le Pen have done and said much worse. But none had ever intimated that they were anything other. The authenticity – the shameless authenticity – is the one real thing. What Mélenchon's supporters have trouble forgiving him for is not the slip ups, but the fact that they are evidence of a mask. Where Trump, or Le Pen might have winked, Mélenchon sulks. He is caught out, and in quite a terminal way.

One way out for FI might be to turn to Mélenchon's faithful lieutenants: Alexis Corbière and, especially, François Ruffin; both of whom enjoy a more authentic image. Ruffin – a documentary film maker – in particular seems to be the party's rising star. More "horizontalist" in contrast to his "Jacobin" boss, Ruffin seems to be poised for success and more able to follow in the footsteps of Five Stars, in terms of disruptive actions (this is not a man who fears confrontation or displays of contempt), but also, to take a page from Marine Le Pen's book, to try and federate slightly different tactics and outlooks under the broad banner of the FI. The French landscape on the left is a field of ruins: to mirror the success of the RN, FI needs to up its authenticity capital. It won't happen under Mélenchon, but, for anyone who can bring in the raw energy of those Gilets Jaunes who declared a sympathy for FI (if not Mélenchon), the field is wide open.

4

Populism goes global: the Netherlands

When I first started paying attention to Dutch politics it was out of a fascination for its capacity to hold itself together despite deep divisions in society. Indeed, the political story of Dutch society is one of institution-building in the face of the constant threat of fragmentation. Much as the low countries had been physically under threat from the sea and built the devices to protect themselves from rising sea-levels, so were they once in danger of disintegration from religious divisions and developed the institutional pillars to defend and define themselves against the forces that could undermine their unity.

My interest was in the nature of these pillars: how they had emerged and managed to structure a peaceful, well-organized coexistence (despite religious differences) and a form of politics defined by negotiation, compromise and elite governance. The system fragmented in the late 1960s and early 1970s and splintered into many more parties, but the continuation of a political culture based on tolerance, openness and compromise seemed ensured.

The Netherlands offered a paradox for sociologists and political analysts: it was a place where there should have been chaos, but where in fact nothing much happened for a very long time (the quip by the nineteenth-century German intellectual Heinrich Heine was that when something did happen, it was 50 years after it had happened anywhere else in the world); and then, in the mid-twentieth century, the Netherlands became a place where almost everything "happened" before it did anywhere else – drug decriminalization, euthanasia, the regulation of prostitution and relaxed attitudes towards diversity of all types. It looked as though even once the old system of pillarized, orderly politics organized around strong, clear (religiously defined) parties had crumbled, the shadow of a form of bourgeois complacency lingered long enough to make the Dutch untroubled with many other aspects of diversity. Bourgeois satisfaction and elite prudence seemed to have seamlessly mutated into Boho acceptance.

So, the early 2000s came as a bit of a shock: in quick succession Pim Fortuyn (an openly gay, anti-Islam, right-wing politician) rose to prominence using a language that broke with Dutch tolerance and compromise. Then Fortuyn was murdered in 2002 (by an environmental activist), just nine days before the general election in which he, and his Lijst Pim Fortuyn party (LPF), were predicted to do well; indeed, his name remained on the ballot, and he ran "posthumously" with LPF capturing 17 per cent of the vote. What followed was a dramatic shift in Dutch public and political discourse, as illustrated by the violent controversies surrounding two outspoken detractors of Islam Ayaan Hirsi Ali and the film maker Theo Van Gogh. The murder of Theo van Gogh in broad daylight, just a couple of years later in November 2004 by an Islamic fundamentalist seemed to seal the change of direction in Dutch politics. By the time Geert Wilders and his Freedom Party exploded onto the national political scene, the Dutch political landscape had already been reshaped by trauma.

A number of questions immediately arose. The first, to do with Fortuyn, was how an educated, openly gay man from Amsterdam could hold, what seemed to most observers, to be such extreme positions against Islam. Fortuyn was well spoken and learned, his views of Islam did not seem to come from run-of-the-mill ignorance or lack of education. He seemed like a very different type of right-wing leader that combined progressive attitudes toward certain forms of diversity (such as homosexuality) with completely reactionary ones toward other forms (such as religious ones). The handy explanation was (as it continues to be for Wilders, as with a new generation of right-wing and left-wing populists) that they are critical of Islam because it clashes with the progressive "ideals" of "the West" (homosexuality and feminism to name a few), although this requires certain contortions on behalf of most of these movements and their leaders, who are usually better known for their ultra-conservative views on homosexuality, women's rights and the family.

The second question that immediately resonated across Europe, and parts of the world, was how, in a place celebrated for its tolerance and capacity to reach compromise, a rhetoric as violent and blunt as Fortuyn's had been able to take root? On various occasions, Fortuyn referred to

Islam as "a backward culture", adding that "there is no freedom in Islam", or that "we must stand together against Islamisation. We must speak the truth and defend our civilisation. If we fail to do so we will end up either enslaved or dead".[1] And other pronouncements designed quite explicitly to break with conventional Dutch political language, and to draw attention not just to difference, but to a kind of incompatibility with fundamental Dutch political values ("Muslims have a very bad attitude to homosexuality. They're very intolerant"). It was, apparently, Muslim intolerance of tolerance that was intolerable.

Fortuyn's discourse was one of the first instances of the widespread use of a discriminatory potential that did not rest on the superiority of race, but on the superiority of cultural development: something hard-won and that could not easily be sacrificed on the altar of multiculturalism. In fact, Dutch tolerance could only thrive if Islam's incompatibility with multicultural attitudes was unmasked. The accusation was that Muslims were prisoners of a culture that was antithetical to Dutch culture.

What could possibly have ushered in such a change in attitudes? Had the Netherlands undergone a fundamental transformation, or were they, momentarily, in the throes of a particular national trauma that would slowly allow for something different to emerge in its wake? A number of things should help answer some of these questions and also explain why "the Dutch case" is a particularly revealing and important one for the story of populism, and that of European populism in particular.

For many analysts, given the Dutch propensity to trail blaze in social and political matters, the question was also whether Wilders would carve out a particular, and longstanding, niche for these politics on the European continent. And I would argue that the transformation of the Dutch political landscape at the turn of the twenty-first century, does in fact lay a trail of crumbs for subsequent developments in European populist politics.

---

1. Among the many examples, see his speech at the Four Seasons Hotel, New York, 23 February 2009; available at: https://www.geertwilders.nl/in-de-media-mainmenu-74/interviews-mainmenu-76/87-english/news/1535-speech-geert-wilders-new-york-four-seasons-monday-feb-23-2009; his interview in *Contemporary Review* in March 2008, available at: https://www.thefreelibrary.com/Geert+Wilders%3a+an+interview+with+the+Netherlands%27+controversial...-a0205111713; and his interview in the *Washington Times* in 2012, available at: https://www.washingtontimes.com/news/2012/sep/14/geert-wilders-5-questions-with-decker/.

In 2004 Geert Wilders was expelled from the VVD (the People's Party for Freedom and Democracy) for having co-authored, with the anti-Islam ideologue and activist Ayaan Hirsi Ali, a pamphlet entitled "The time has come for a liberal Jihad". In it they advocated the suspension of the constitutional rights of Dutch Muslims. Wilders had form: earlier that year he had called for the deportation of all radical Muslims from the Netherlands. As a result of his expulsion, Wilders went on to found his own party, the Party for Freedom (PVV), and in 2006 it won 5.9 per cent of the vote. In 2010 it won 15 per cent of the vote and supported the VVD/CDA minority coalition government (and although it never formally joined it, it contributed to bringing it down and triggering early elections); in 2012 it paid a price for what was considered its reckless behaviour in bringing down the government and only attained 10 per cent of the vote. In 2017 it was once again at 13 per cent: the second party in the Netherlands, albeit a distant second.

Wilders and the circumstances that enabled his rise are of particular relevance for the argument of this book: Wilders marks a turning point in the language and posture of populism. With him, despite his anti-Islam stance, populism takes a decisive step away from traditional far-right ideologies by embracing a set of much more contemporary voter concerns to do with everyday life, but also – against the background of the 9/11 attacks – a perceived loss of control over their everyday environments, and more to the point, exploiting their growing infatuation with authenticity and transparency as weapons against a process of globalization that they were beginning to increasingly resent.

Transparency

The Netherlands are particularly interesting because it is a political culture based, on the one hand, on a highly elitist form of bargaining – that was, in essence, opaque to ordinary people – but also reliant on highly publicized rules and rituals designed to deliver stability and continuity in the face of potential religious and political strife. The formula was transparent, whereas the cooking, like Bismarck's sausages and constitutions, was kept under wraps. In this situation it is no wonder that transparency has remained a strong currency in Dutch politics: the system relies on everyone knowing the rules, knowing their place, and knowing how to play the game. This is an important point because of the four case studies, the Netherlands is the only one in which political culture is based on transparency. This combination makes the Netherlands a particularly hospitable host for contemporary populism: transparency and bluntness are prized; relying on unspoken rules is valued, but at the same time, the ingrained tendency toward elite bargaining was a perfect foil for discontent (what are they doing behind our backs?). Enter Wilders and Fortuyn.

Open curtains and normality

A metaphor that came up repeatedly in the various research projects I carried out in the Netherlands, was that of the Dutch street in which no household closes its curtains in the evening. Not because the Dutch venerate nosiness, but, as was explained to me countless times, because there should be nothing in your house that you would want to hide. Being good meant being accessible, readable and without secrets. A window, much like a Vermeer, should serve as a frame for an ordinary and modest life.

The metaphor of the "open curtains" cuts in a number of enlightening ways. First, it suggests a deep commitment to bringing life down to the smallest, most familiar and domestic scale. The more domestic and bite-sized the ritual, the more it is cherished. It reminded me of something a Dutch friend once said as I extolled the virtues of his homeland and its openness and tolerance: he nodded and then added, "although you have to understand that we cannot deal with any debate that doesn't fit in our front rooms. The fact that we seem to be so at ease with these large issues is because we cut them down to size, strip them of any grand, moral meaning and deal with them as though they were breakfast choices".

Beyond the danger of reducing social and political choices to a matter of the household, the open curtains imply a second important thing: the curtains may be proof that you have nothing to hide – which was the explanation I was given – but they also imply that you are immediately knowable. Not only are Dutch households open, but anyone who peers in has the capacity to make sense of the scene. This instant understanding of one another – and the mourning of its passing – is a recurring theme in the conversations in the Netherlands, but also elsewhere.

The broken spell of a silent consensus

In conversations when I suggested that, perhaps it was a matter of explaining such mores, so as to give anyone new to Dutch society a chance to fit in and integrate, the reaction was always the same: but why should I have to explain? It should be obvious. Often, in fact, it was the very notion of having to put into words what should be wordless, that was thought to be most disturbing. This was particularly true of conversations in the Netherlands, but also in Finland and Sweden: two other consensual democracies where this silent understanding was seen as crucial to the sense of nationhood.

One of the key insights from the Netherlands was just how reluctant people were to have to explain themselves; and part of it was that they were reluctant to spell out "the obvious". But part of it was something else, it was growing unease with conversation and dialogue. Dialogue had come to mean, to many of the people I spoke to, bending over backwards to make themselves understandable, when in fact they had not changed.[2]

There is a paradox here about the spoken word. On the one hand the many Dutch people I spoke to valued an unspoken, instant understanding of one another – of people "like them". On the other, however, they valued the bluntness of what they said. And, more to the point, they valued a society where you could say what you thought as bluntly as you liked, secure in the knowledge that you would not be misunderstood. So, while the debate could be had, the rules of the debate were not up for discussion.

Multiculturalism was often seen here as having conspired against this openness: as in many other contexts, the accusation was that multiculturalism had allowed the harbouring of enemies of Dutch political culture in the Netherlands, forbidding people to call them out on it in the name of tolerance. Fortuyn was forever referring to the naivety of those who thought that you could let Islam evolve into a force for good; giving what he referred to as "the benefit of the doubt" was a mistake. As for Theo Van Gogh he made his name denouncing what he thought

---

2. See Counterpoint's "The Threats of Populism: Europe's Reluctant Radicals" project, http://counterpoint.uk.com/ideaslab/reluctant-radicals-2/ (accessed 22 March 2019) and Fieschi 2013.

was the hypocrisy of elites and their tolerance of the intolerable. For many in the Netherlands who subsequently turned to Wilders, the two murders demonstrated that multiculturalism was a set of practices that, by requiring that people *not* call a spade a spade and bury their aversions and fears in the name of an equality of cultures, had unleashed violence. The murders of Fortuyn and van Gogh forced the emergence of a particular argument, namely that it was multiculturalism, with its demands for politeness and unconditional acceptance, that was anathema to the inherent progressiveness of Dutch political culture (thus leading Wilders to argue a few years later "We are fed up with the elites, who offer you a beautiful ideal world, in which all cultures are morally equivalent").

In this respect Dutch populism was a trail-blazer: First, because it mounted a critique of multiculturalism as the most important symptom of a politics that was inauthentic. All of multiculturalism's basic tenets (that one needs to learn tolerance, that one can create institutions that can turn diversity into an asset, that language needs to be practiced carefully and used in order to accommodate and respect diversity) were taken as the signs of an intellectual posturing clearly at odds with common sense, but more to the point with instinct. The very fact that one needed to be told this was for Dutch populists (politicians and voters) the proof that it was at odds with the true values of the real Dutch. Second, because it fed the populist paradigm of the protection of progressive values. This attitude, that one did not condemn Muslims out of racism, but Islam precisely out of progressivism emerged particularly virulently in the Netherlands. But Wilders took it global. Finally, Wilders trail-blazed in the sense that he allowed himself a bluntness that was spectacular (even by Dutch standards) and that infected the rest of European politics. While Jean-Marie Le Pen was making anti-Semitic jokes – a subject that was always controversial – Wilders broke taboos. And said what no one had ever said – in public – in the Netherlands.

The two murders reinforced the perception that what was at stake was the Dutch capacity to live with difference because difference was not buried or denied, but rather exposed and managed, and that multiculturalism with its euphemisms and dissimulation was inauthentic, and therefore not suited to Dutch political culture.

What is striking is how many of populism's core ideas are core to Dutch political culture. The paradox if there is one, is the fact that it took so long for an ideology based in part on authenticity and democracy to emerge. But the two murders changed that. And although they could be characterized as the result of existing populism, the more likely explanation is that they were seen as a consequence of the betrayal of authentic Dutch values by the elites, who had not bothered to protect two authentic Dutch voices.

The context of trauma

The interplay between outspokenness and the value placed on immediate understanding is lent an added dimension by the trauma induced by the murders of Fortuyn and Van Gogh. There is no overstating the national shock that followed. Nor should anyone underestimate the manner in which they shaped the public response to the growth of Dutch populist politics, and Wilders in particular. And the manner in which this reaction has helped to configure European populism in the years since.

I recall a university seminar a few years later (one of many) that brought into focus the difficulty of discussing populism in the Netherlands. In the context of a progressive and educated assembly, the discussion – which was meant to revolve around how to deal with populist politics in ways that would lead to diffusing social and political tensions and reducing Wilders' capacity to inflame and polarize politics to the point of stalemate – regularly ground to a halt as those of us who were not Dutch attempted to formulate the terms in which to call into question the validity of Wilders' views. It was impossible. The consensus in the room (in all of the rooms) was against criticism. The refrain was that voting for Wilders was a "perfectly legitimate political option" and there should be no opprobrium linked to it. After many months of this, I finally cornered some Dutch colleagues in a bar and asked, bluntly, why they refused to be even a little bit more critical of Wilders' politics? Why it seemed so impossible, to refrain from, of course, judging the voters (the distinction between the supporters of populist parties and the parties/leaders themselves should always be borne in mind), but to nevertheless point out, at least, that voting for such politics rarely delivered what the voters thought they needed. That their grievances should be heard, but that the solutions they proposed, by way of supporting

Wilders, might still be questioned. Every time I asked, the answer came swiftly and invariably: because if we condemn outspoken views, look at what happens: things get violent. Populist politics was essentially a safety valve to deal with the collective trauma of the murders. It was in the aftermath of a number of these discussions that it became clear that the violence (both physical and verbal) that marked the rise of populism and inaugurated it, as it were, with two murders, would continue to shape the Dutch public's capacity to react to it.

Indeed, in one conversation in April 2012 (again, post-seminar), one Dutch colleague asked how long our research team was going to be in town. When I replied that we were leaving the next day, he said it was too bad because we would be missing the memorial for Pim Fortuyn marking the 10 years since his assassination. I agreed, that it would have been an interesting research piece to carry out, possibly rich in conversations and interviews. His reply however was that, it would be good to "pay respects". I was a little surprised and asked whether he was suggesting that Fortuyn was a hero. His reply was characteristic: not a hero, he said, but someone worthy of respect.

It is worth thinking about these two traumatic events and the way in which they directly shaped Dutch populist politics, and populism well beyond the Netherlands. The reactions across the board seem to indicate deep guilt: a deep sense of responsibility. For those who had supported multiculturalism, they felt that it was time to let people express themselves and bluntly, and as freely as they wanted. Better that than a growing hidden violence – this was the equivalent of pulling back the curtains. As a result little condemnation followed. For those who had felt ill at ease with it, it was a signal that they could indeed be more critical, speak without filters, be blunter and more aggressive. The outcome is a situation in which trauma justifies both the glorification of outspokenness as well as the native culture of wordless understanding. It explains in part why, in conjunction with broader cultural developments and the rise of digital, it was so easy for Wilders to make headway.

The Netherlands and the great populist turn

It is a cliché to argue that the world changed between 2000 and 2003 – the attacks on New York and on the Pentagon, and the concatenation of events to which they gave rise reshaped the world. Traumas cascaded in quick succession: 9/11, the Iraq war, and 7/7 in London (not to mention the unfolding of events further afield). The murders in Amsterdam, about which Buruma (2006) wrote, are nestled within that period. They contribute to the remaking of populism. Indeed, they contribute to its flight and transformation into an ideology. In this respect the Netherlands are what one might call "the hinge": developments in the Netherlands (from Fortuyn, to Wilders and via van Gogh) mark the moment at which, given the confluence of specific events, deep European and global transformations, and the increase in the ubiquity of digital in our lives, populism starts to transform itself into a powerful ideology. This would reshape populism across Europe.

The Wilders turn

By the time Geert Wilders was expelled from the VVD in 2004, the atmosphere in the Netherlands was ripe for his promises. Building on the murders and atmosphere of resentment against multiculturalism and on the demands for a return to the "plain talk" of traditional Dutch politics, Wilders created the PVV in 2006 with the explicit intention of "limiting the number of Muslims in the Netherlands". The party was explicitly and stridently anti-migrant, and specifically anti-Islam: it campaigned on promises to stop the Islamization of the Netherlands and to ban the Koran (which Wilders repeatedly compared to Hitler's *Mein Kampf*).

In many respects, the PVV built on classic populist themes of migration, "Us vs Them", the real people versus a corrupt and careless elite. The latter was admirably documented by Ian Buruma who writes: "there was something unhinged about the Netherlands in the winter of 2004. And I wanted to understand it better" (Buruma 2006: 10). Most importantly, Buruma outlines the complacency of the Dutch elite and its consequences: "The politics of consensus contains its own forms of corruption: politics gets stuck in the rut of a self-perpetuating elite, shuffling jobs back and forth between members of the club". He also refers to the "look of quiet self-satisfaction" acquired simply as a result of running a small nation where "all people of consequence know one another" (*ibid.*: 46–9). Above all, Buruma describes a country complacent toward stratification and exclusion. Until it could be complacent no more.

Exclusion, in various guises, comes up again and again in conversations. When I was carrying out research into the attitudes of Wilders' supporters (and more broadly, Dutch citizens who seemed seduced by the harder rhetoric and ideas of right-wing populism), a number of stories recurred. One was that of the "decline of the polder spirit". Many of the ordinary citizens I spoke to in the context of this research – whatever their political views – referred to a deep sense of loss. For many this was about a loss of innocence, a loss of their own tolerance and humanistic culture, and their capacity to get along and reach consensus through working out problems together. The polders – those flat, open lands reclaimed from the sea – were the symbol of what the Dutch had been able to build together by forging, or recognizing, a common interest. For others, however, the polders had come to symbolize a consensus from which they felt excluded: in those cases "poldering" was referred to as a kind of stitch-up, in which people who pretended to be adversaries, really had a lot more in common than they admitted publicly, while leaving the non-elite out in the cold.

This "stitch-up" was a source of growing resentment. And went hand in hand with the perceived loss of an equality of status and a modesty, fundamental to Dutch politics. The polders might have kept the Netherlands safe, but they were now held to be either a thing of the past, or a manipulative mirage. For the former, the question was what the Dutch could still build together to create a sense of unity. For those who held the latter opinion, it was a question of moving on, being honest and being blunt about the short-comings of the polder model.

Breaking the spell and restoring authentic politics

Fortuyn, Van Gogh, Wilders were respected in part because they broke the silence around the fact that the game was rigged: that not everyone's voice was equally valuable, and that shaping the consensus had become the prerogative of an elite, which was only pretending to engage in debate. What followed was an unleashing of forces that had perhaps been stirring for a long time.

But aside from the emphasis on immigration, integration, and in particular Islam, what characterizes Wilders' approach is his emphasis on authenticity and transparency, and on the clear-eyed understanding that populist leaders and their supporters bring to politics. Much of Wilders' discourse is an appeal to a desacralization of liberal language. Indeed his words are so over-the-top, they are such a deluge of anti-liberal, anti-tolerant sentiment that they are almost a caricature. The enormity of the onslaught hasn't been properly transmitted by the foreign press. Offensive expressions are given as examples here and there, but it takes a full paragraph of a speech to get the proper measure of what is being said:

> This government, this elite, does not have the slightest will to resist [...] Islamization [...]. All those cosy mosques, all those nice headscarves, all those snug burqas: they really make the Netherlands a lot prettier. Here and there someone drops dead, occasionally someone gets raped, and the country is going bankrupt at some point, but that cannot spoil the fun. That is mere detail. Just be patient for a little longer, and then the Islamic utopia awaits us. A better environment begins with you. A great many Dutch people are annoyed at the pollution of public space by Islam. In other words, in certain places our street scene more and more resembles the street scene in Mecca or Tehran: headscarves, *"haardbaarden"* (the so-called "fireplace beards"), burqas, and men in weird long white dresses. Let us do something about that for once. Let us reconquer our streets. Let us ensure that the Netherlands is finally going to resemble the Netherlands again. Those headscarves really are a symbol of female oppression, a sign of subjection, a sign of conquest. They form a symbol of an ideology that intends to colonize us. Therefore, the time has come for a great cleaning of our streets. If our *"nieuwe Nederlanders"* like to show their love for this seventh-century desert ideology, they should do so in an Islamic country, but not here. Not in the Netherlands. The Netherlands has excise taxes. We have excises on gas and diesel. We have excises on parking. We have excises on dogs. We used to have excises on flying. We still have excises on packaging materials. My first proposal: why not the introduction of a headscarf tax? I would like to call it a *kopvoddentaks*. Just get a permit once a year and pay right away. A thousand euros a year seems like a nice amount to me. Then we will finally earn

back a little of what has already cost us so much. I would say: the polluter pays.[3]

The climax of the piece is of course the proposed "headscarf tax"; as noted by commentators at the time, the very word "*kopvoddentaks*" is onomatopoeic – it sounds spat out. That ending is also a symbolic tipping point into something absurd, indeed grotesque, with the suggested €1,000 a year as the tax rate. The point here is a vocabulary that is designed to be liberating in its outrageousness: it combines ethnic cleansing, a call to violence, and the appropriation of various liberal slogans ("the polluter pays", or "a better environment begins with you"). It is all there and calculated to provide maximum release through maximum bombast and bravado. It is 100 per cent authentically transparent and offensive, nothing is hidden. It is worth noting that the 2006 election manifesto was entitled "Straight talk".[4]

This "politics of offence", is designed to restore people's right and capacity to see through the spell cast by elites and multiculturalism. It is an exhortation to become authentically Dutch once again. Wilders' propaganda video *Fitna* (2008) is another case in point: in the first half of the video is a mix of recitations from the Koran and violent cartoons (the bombings in London and Madrid, the assassination of Theo van Gogh, a plane flying into the World Trade Centre) and it ends with the words "Hitler was right". The second half opens with the heading, "The Netherlands under the spell of Islam" and the prophet Muhammad is depicted as a cartoon with a ticking time-bomb turban. The fact that *Fitna* in many ways mimics Jihadist propaganda videos is no accident.

The point is four-fold: first, nothing is off limits because Wilders as a true Dutchman is rebelling against the shackles of multiculturalism and returning to the roots of political culture in the Netherlands; secondly, as a leader it is his duty to "red-pill" (i.e. impart his harsh but necessary

---

3. Wilders made these comments on 16 September 2009 during a parliamentary debate on the budget.

4. This is a version of what Herbert Marcuse referred to as "repressive desublimation": the encouragement to be as blunt and un-PC as possible in order to provoke the media and opponents, and to signal to his supporters that it is acceptable to use offensive and vulgar language. Often with a hint of humour or sarcasm. For an excellent discussion of Wilders' language, see Bot 2017.

knowledge) Dutch citizens, and exhort them to re-become themselves – to wake from the spell (to be "woke" as the American Alt-Right puts it); thirdly, the subtext is "we understand each other", we get the joke about the headscarf tax, we get the joke about the slogans – no explanation is needed. Finally, there is nothing here that cannot be admitted to because it is who we are: no offence can be taken because one cannot be offended by expressions of authenticity.

Wilders' insistence on indoctrination is yet another clue as to the aims of his rhetoric; to dis-inhibit his fellow citizens, because they are who they are, and have nothing to be ashamed of:

> One of the things we are no longer allowed to say is that our culture is superior to certain other cultures. [...] We are inundated with feelings of guilt and shame about our own identity and what we stand for. We are exhorted to respect everyone and everything, except ourselves. That is the message of the Left and the politically-correct ruling establishment. They want us to feel so ashamed about our own identity that we refuse to fight for it. ... we must stop feeling guilty about who we are. We are not "kafir", we are not guilty.[5]

The populism that emerges from these events in the Netherlands acts as the gateway to contemporary forms by shaping the acceptable language of populism and ushering in a different kind of ideology, bound up with both external events (terrorism) and new forms of communications that re-design citizen expectations and their relationship to institutions and politics more broadly. Multiculturalism comes under attack, Islam more directly comes under attack, and language undergoes a fundamental transformation in that the racism is rooted in a defence of the West, a defence of tolerance, a defence of values, and of the West as tolerant and progressive places rather than in the rhetoric of superiority and inferiority linked to classical racism. And this in the context of great trauma to the West as its symbols are attacked: 9/11 and in the case of the Netherlands the murders of Fortuyn and Van Gogh.

---

5. Geert Wilders, speech at Hotel Berlin, Berlin, 2 October 2010; available at https://www.pvv.nl/36-fj-related/geert-wilders/3586-speech-geert-wilders-berlijn.html (accessed 22 March 2019).

The reactions of the Dutch are also amongst the first to be broadcast via social media. Whereas the populism of Le Pen came into the world as memory's last hurrah, the populism of the Netherlands, and the one that Dutch politics ushers in via Wilders and unleashes upon Europe and elsewhere, comes into the world blinking in the glare from a set of traumas that wipe out the past, and in a world of social media that promises a never-ending present and new illusions.

5

Populism's poster child? Italy

I grew up in northern Italy in the 1970s and my memories are of an incomprehensible mixture of complete inertia – Nothing. Ever. Changed. – and permanent upheaval. Food was predictable, Sundays were predictable, church was predictable, school was stultifying. But what was also predictable were bombings, assassinations and kidnappings. I remember General Dalla Chiesa coming to dinner and landing by helicopter on the roof of our building (and believe me, there was no helipad up there), surrounded by carabinieri to protect him from the Red Brigades – which he eventually vanquished, only to be murdered along with his young wife by the mafia in Parlermo in 1982. In 1992 it was the turn of Judge Falcone, and then a few short months later, Judge Borsellino was also murdered. And in between, there was the kidnapping and killing of Aldo Moro. This mix of predictability and, often violent, turmoil, is the backdrop against which contemporary Italian populism arises.

Deep roots

Getting to the roots of Italian populism sometimes feels like a problem of infinite regress. From today's coalition government between the right-wing populist Lega and the left-wing populist Five Star Movement (M5S), you take a step back to Silvio Berlusconi and the 1990s; which takes you remarkably quickly back to the immediate postwar moment and the "uomo qualunque" movement ("movement of the ordinary man"); which then takes you back to fascism (and its inescapable populist component). At which point someone stops you and says that you really need to go back to the "southern question". What about 1860 and unification then? Much further back, comes the answer.

First, the so-called southern question and the disparity of wealth between the North of Italy and the poorer South, which became even starker after unification (in the 1860s) as more efficient northern manufacturers and their less efficient southern counterparts came into direct competition, is undoubtedly significant. All current regionalist debates have their origins in this period, and regionalist debates underpin Italian politics; they continue to be an ever-present and structuring set of dynamics.

Second, fascism and its legacy are important. Italian fascism and Mussolini's regime play a role in the entrenchment of populism on the Italian political landscape. Mussolini's mobilization of populist rhetoric through his newspaper, *Il popolo d'Italia* ("The People of Italy"), propagated an "Us vs. Them" dichotomy. He purported to represent ordinary Italians against the bankers and industrialists, regarded as the new aristocracy, whose interests were served by parliamentary democracy. Instead, Mussolini proposed "trenchocracy", a system that valued those who had fought in the trenches of the First World War above their compatriots. This developed into a militaristic, authoritarian regime, but one which also demonstrated the potential of populism. I have written about this elsewhere (Fieschi 2004), but my contention is that while it is certainly easy to overemphasize Mussolini's direct influence on current politics, populism's key concepts do play a part in the ideology of fascism.[1]

And while Italy's postwar settlement was born of a reaction against the fascist regime, populism reinfected Italian politics as soon as the Second World War ended through the Sicilian independence movement, that brought renewed vigour to the "us" (Sicilians) vs "them" (Italians) distinction based on North/South relations. From Sicily these ideas were exported to Naples and then to Rome thanks to ship-owner and Rome Mayor Achille Lauro. Lauro's claim was that if these large southern cities were poor and underdeveloped, it was the fault of the greedy, corrupt, industralized northern elite. The mobilization around these issues was translated at national level in the immediate aftermath

---

1. They provide a bridge between the seemingly contradictory elitism and the egalitarian collective appeal of much fascist doctrine. Populism is partly what grants fascism its more social aspects, thereby leading some scholars to declare it "neither right nor left".

of the war by Guglielmo Giannini's "Front of the Ordinary Man". You can see the trail of breadcrumbs.

Finally, the actual nature of postwar Italy is consequential. The period of Italian history that begins in 1946 and is lazily characterized as one of chronic instability (52 governments in 48 years) actually dissimulates a more powerful reality. Beneath the instability, there is the very opposite: inertia and a completely ossified political system. The largest party in every government coalition during the First Republic was Democrazia Cristiana (DC), and the level of ministerial reappointment from one government to the next was extremely high.[2] In this "*immobilismo*" as Italians characterized it, nothing really changed for nearly half a century.

Mirroring the domination of DC and its various and varying allies in government was the total hegemony of the communist opposition Partito Comunista Italiano (PCI). The result was one of the most highly polarized, bipolar political systems in Europe. But which enabled DC to build and maintain support given the perceived threat of the communist alternative, as well as the constant insinuation that good Catholics could only be seen to participate in politics via Christian Democratic parties (let's not forget that the Vatican actually discouraged political participation well into the 1930s). By gradually capturing the institutions of the Italian state, DC fostered a system of deep and extensive clientelism. It was not until the 1980s that its position began to weaken, when reports of political and administrative corruption finally undermined the party's ability to mobilize voters, even by buying them off. Electoral volatility increased dramatically and the result was the emergence of a number of protest parties: the Radical party, the Greens and, in the late-1980s, the Northern Leagues (for there were several at the time). The combination of the collapse of the Soviet Union in the early 1990s and the resulting disintegration of Italy's communist party, led to the end of Italy's famed *partitocrazia* (rule by parties) and the demise of its First Republic.

---

2. Calise & Mannheimer (1992) show that in the first 30 years of the regime, 37 ministers had served in at least five cabinets, whilst several had been involved in 12 cabinets, and one minister had served in 30. The persistence ratio between cabinets – that is, the number of ministers who retained a cabinet position between governments – was calculated at 57.7 per cent between 1946 and 1976.

So when in February 1992, Judge Antonio di Pietro sanctioned the arrest of Mario Chiesa, a politician in the Partito Socialista Italiano (PSI), on charges of receiving a bribe from a Milanese cleaning company, the Italian system was ripe for not just a clean-out, but also a deep restructuring that would be fuelled, in part, by the proto-populisms that had in fact been nurtured since the end of the war. The accusations triggered what became known as *Mani pulite* ("clean hands"), a nation-wide judicial investigation into widespread corruption. By the end of 1993 many politicians had become embroiled in the affair, including 251 MPs, with four former prime ministers, five ex-party leaders and seven former cabinet members among them. By then ten suspects had taken their own lives.

It was this convergence of several specific conditions – in this field of political ruins – that created the optimum circumstances for the rise of a contemporary form of populism: a sustained lack of political alter-nation (*immobilismo*), the undue influence of parties within the demo-cratic system (*partitocrazia*), the subsequent and sudden peak in judicial oversight (*Mani pulite*), and the sudden disappearance of the two main established parties – the PCI, and the DC – as well as the dissolution of the PSI. In 1993, an eight-question referendum was held to determine the public's views on a range of issues, including the adoption of a new electoral process for the Senate, the abolition of some government min-istries and the repeal of regulations on party financing. Despite a lack of substantive constitutional change (more *immobilismo*), this is generally considered to be the beginning of the Italian Second Republic. The lack of institutional change, or rather, the lack of any perceptible change in everyday politics in the aftermath of 1994 has to be taken into account: the return to normal (corruption, nepotism, poor services) was in many ways the broken promise that broke the Italian camel's back. The result of course, was more populist politics, not less.

The Second Republic: populism centre stage?

The Second Italian Republic has seen the transformation and emergence of several significant populist or proto-populist forces, which, in the end, have been more successful than many of their European counter-parts, in terms of the duration and breadth of their electoral support, as well as access to high office. The trajectories of the main Italian populist protagonists (for the sake of argument let's include Berlusconi's Forza Italia because of the important role it plays, but certainly the Lega[3] and the Five Star Movement) and their organizational structures have been varied. Over time these forces evolved in two ways: they gradually emancipated themselves from the North–South divide and their strong autonomist/nationalist movement flavours; and they steadily developed a tone and rhetoric that emphasized a completely different relationship to voters.

Berlusconi and TV politics

The year 1994 marks the refoundation of the Italian party system, and at the time many worried about the vacuum left on the moderate and conservative side. Gianni Agnelli, president of Fiat was repeatedly courted to run for the premiership. Agnelli turned it down, but came up with the idea of asking Silvio Berlusconi.

Berlusconi, who was born in Milan in 1936 to a wealthy middle-class family, had the kind of ordinary, yet colourful past that would appeal to the citizens of a nation fed up with machine politics; with his crooner background (he sang on cruise ships in the 1960s) and real entrepreneurial flair, Berlusconi ticked a lot of boxes. He was a new face, he sounded congenial, but above all, in 1993 Berlusconi was Italy's richest man (see Stille 2010). He owned Mediaset (a media empire that included television stations and advertising agencies), Fininvest (a financial and business empire that included enormous property developments), a network of cinemas, and the football club, AC Milan. The fact that he used television so effectively (many remember his initial broadcast in 1994, dubbed "Getting onto the pitch" because he used the football expression repeatedly), and his media and finance (Fininvest) empire so ruthlessly (to push out the message, to poll voters, and to shape the political narrative), set him apart immediately. Others had captured some of the state

---

3. Originally known as the Lega Lombarda, before joining a coalition with other northern regionalist parties to form the Lega Nord in 1991, the party became known as the Lega for the 2018 general elections under the leadership of Matteo Salvini. This was an attempt to build nationwide support for the party, rather than confine its political activity to the North of Italy.

apparatus, and sometimes captured parts of the press, but no one had controlled such an effective network and potential electoral machine: one that could both *broadcast* information out, as well as *collect* information about what Italians liked to consume. It was the perfect political vehicle. And well aware of what Italians consumed more than anything (television and football), his movement's name, was no more than a football cheer: Forza Italia! (Go Italy!). He assembled his party much as one would assemble a company or a football team: by setting up a structure, appointing its board and hiring employees, and then behaving as CEO and Chairman all rolled into one (Riotta 2013: 594).

Paul Heywood and I have written about "entrepreneurial populism" (Fieschi & Heywood 2004). We have argued that the reasoning behind a vote for someone like Berlusconi might go something like this: "although the system may be corrupt, the appropriate response is to vote for someone who can play this system to the mutual advantage of voter and candidate" (*ibid.*: 303). Berlusconi had clearly known how to make the system work to his advantage, yet he was a true outsider in political terms. The point was that neither the voters nor the leaders were particularly trusting of each other, this was a cynical alliance in its purest form – a political transaction. But one that many Italians thought would finally bring something new to the table. The cynicism of the alliance is worth highlighting here, for reasons we hinted at earlier. Berlusconi's emergence came after a period of huge turbulence: an inert system characterized by corruption and political violence gave way to a new political deal. The moment held a promise of dynamism and renewal, but also of stability and even serenity to replace the constant threats to the civil peace. When Berlusconi entered politics in 1994, he certainly did not have a choir-boy reputation (although like most Italian boys, he would probably have been one at some point), but his success in business really was taken as a promise that he would help Italy flourish, in the way that his own media and business empire had. The hope was not a naïve expectation of irreproachable politics, it was slightly more cynical and also more real. Not a pact with the devil just yet, but a pact with "*un furbo*" – someone with street-smarts and experience, likely to deliver the goods. This was the umpteenth bargain of this kind struck by Italians, and not the last. There are two reasons why this matters: first, because Berlusconi does mark a tipping point which explains the situation in early 2019 and the coalition of the Lega and the Five Star Movement; and, secondly, because so many dashed hopes and bad deals explain the near-hysterical tone of Italian populist parties – a combination of outrage, insults, accusations rarely seen outside of Trump's America.

One first key point to note is that Berlusconi's language and style evolved very quickly. This is potentially because his decision to participate in politics was followed by almost immediate political success (indeed, Berlusconi entered politics in January of 1994, and was elected in March of 1994 as the head of a coalition that included both the Lega Nord and the post-fascist Alleanza Nazionale). Whilst the 1994 "Scendere in campo" televised address was a fairly traditional liberal, anti-left declaration that spoke much of freedom, of the free market and of the right to a good job, by 1998, the tone was far more cavalier, relaxed about the dysfunctionalities of the Italian political system, and consistently against any reforms that might get in the way of his business interests.

The populism of the CEO?

Berlusconi is an almost unfathomable paradox. On the one hand, he represents a form of continuity, fitting into a long line of corrupt Italian politicians, playing the system for their own political and personal gain (and it is worth keeping in mind that he was prime minister four times and holds the record for the longest political tenure in Italy). This is a politician who used every known trick in the Italian politics handbook and every available channel to pursue his own interest to the direct detriment of Italy and its citizens (changing laws in his favour, and bankrupting key groups with catastrophic consequences for Italy's balance sheet and for its workers).

On the other hand, Berlusconi helped – amidst the complete wipe out of the First Republic – to catapult Italy into a new political era. He may have been pushed to set it up, but the party was entirely his own creation; it came out of nowhere and, despite the nature of the set-up, centred entirely on him – it was a personal vehicle (while it is tempting to reach for fascism as a comparator, the fact is that Mussolini created his various iterations of the National Fascist Party out of pre-existing movements). Berlusconi's use of language was also entirely new, calibrated to resonate as broadly as possible, and studded with football and television show references and metaphors.

And the paradox does not let up. Seen from one angle, Berlusconi is classic populism. He uses key populist ideas: the hammered message that he was "made of the same stuff" as ordinary people despite his wealth, that he was one of them; that, over and above that, he was a defender of the popular will, albeit very much as the CEO of "Italy Plc" (and as a CEO, had no time to waste on the time-consuming and hollow rituals of parliamentary debate); and finally, as a CEO whose responsibility was to Italian citizens only (not the political class) as his "shareholders". The appeals are to ordinary men and women as they go about their everyday, non-political business, but as individuals, not as citizens. The people he is talking to are not citizens, they are the television viewers, the football fans and the shoppers (Tarchi 2008: 94); those whom he knows and who use his services and products. In many respects this gave Berlusconi the quality of a clever shop-keeper. At best the paternalistic owner of the local factory: connected and powerful but embedded in the community and responsible for its well-being, which is intrinsically connected to his own financial success (so let's not ask too many questions or persecute him with rules and regulations). The genius of Berlusconi was to be able to project this small-town mentality onto an entire country through his personality, but also his media empire.

His use of ordinary language, which he regularly contrasted with "*politichese*" – the language of politics, but also of the chattering classes – and his reliance on common sense as the pivot around which every decision must be made, are key populist tropes. There are no abstract principles, no great ideological appeals, his is a "school of life" kind of political language designed to distance him from what he claims to loathe most – the professional political class, the professional political parties – and build a much more direct bridge to Italian voters. It is interesting to pause here and contrast Berlusconi's relationship to the political class with that of Trump, who is the inevitable comparison. Both businessmen, both claiming to run the country as businessmen would and not as politicians would, with the expectation of expediency and results.

There are however some crucial differences in their approach, which help to highlight why Bersluscoini was, at best, "populism lite". Trump's claims to being an outsider are often contested on the grounds that he is well-connected as someone who is extremely wealthy. But two things are clear: the first is that his contempt for Washington is real. When he says he wants to "drain the swamp", there is no doubt, for better or for worse, both that he believes Washington to be a swamp, and that he wants to drain it. The second, is that he did surround himself mainly with people who had little professional experience of politics, certainly of Washington politics. This was not the case at all with Berlusconi. He may have had no direct experience in politics, but he was supremely well-connected in traditional Christian Democratic circles; and he surrounded himself with professionals from those circles when he was elected. Finally, at no point did Berlusconi try to reform or change Italian political dynamics in any way beyond what he needed to get away with his own fraud. Trump may be trying to do that, but what he is also doing is trying to implement a completely different vision of the United States, its role in the world and its priorities, and he has true contempt for Washington and its "system" (from the media, to the bureaucracy). While in no way endorsing that approach, it does suggest an aspiration on the part of Trump to change the United States for motives that include direct personal interest or gain but also go beyond that. In this respect, while much of Trump is a cynical appeal to voters that he doesn't respect in the way he claims to, there is nevertheless a commitment to deep change that – again for better or for worse – is far more authentic than Berlusconi's and much more in line with a populist ideology rooted in control, absolute sovereignty, and non-professional politics.

A final point of comparison takes us back to political appeals: Berlusconi, certainly at the time, was non-ideological; Trump is anything but that. Beyond Trump's ad hominem and personal attacks, there is the near-constant evocation and tackling of highly flammable political issues (security, immigration, foreign policy, etc), on top of the gratuitous rattling of every possible cage. This may be largely for agitation and rabble-rousing purposes; a wish to take up explosive topics in order to set the system alight. But it was completely absent from Berlusconi's repertoire. Aside from the vague impression of toying with a few superficial public service reforms, there was no desire for deep change, or transformation beyond his own protection. And there was certainly no deep appeal to the people. Even the slogan Forza Italia! can be taken in two ways (and the various clips of Berlusconi are a vivid illustration of this): it can be a rallying cry (of the "Make American Great Again" kind, or Salvini's "Italians First!"), but just as often it is spoken as gentle encouragement: *forza Italia* – without the exclamation mark – "come on

Italy ... just a little extra push, you can do it". There is very little here, to suggest the kind of appeal to a highly mobilized – or mobilizable – Italian people. As discussed previously, if there is one thing that binds together populist leaders and parties it is their shared conception of the people: one that is relatively organic but also transcendent, to form the nation, especially on the right. Even ordinariness is conceived of as metaphysical: deeply rooted in a quasi-mystical cultural and geographical whole.

Berlusconi never hits those populist high notes – he doesn't appeal to the nation, or to an imagined and idealized demos, but rather positions himself as a fixer and a stabilizer; no major promises of change, just hints that things might gradually improve. Unless the boat was rocked for him, Berlusconi had no desire to do so; no desire to accomplish anything by doing so. Mainly, it was about getting the system to work for him. You might argue that whereas Trump is trying to take the *Art of the Deal* to politics, Berlusconi was always applying the art of politics to his deals. The result is very different and accounts, partly, for the way in which Berlusconi was able to embed himself in the Italian political landscape, whereas Trump can only play disruptor on a grand scale.

Reshaping Italy: the politics of real fakeness

In many respects, with his bombast and his crassness, Berlusconi, was the first to usher in that distorted transparency that is the hallmark of contemporary populism. The charade of honesty did not last much beyond 1994; quickly the world was faced with someone whose, "I am like you", meant "I can be as bad as anyone". Plagued by sexual scandal and accusations of corruption, infamous for his vanity (the hair-plugs, the face-lifts, the perma-tan, the claims to sexual prowess), his edifice nevertheless finally came tumbling down with the Ruby Robacuore scandal (when he was accused of having a sexual relationship with an under-age prostitute), his wife's belated desertion, and the guilty verdict of the Italian courts, and a ban on running for office (now lifted of course).

What is interesting, is how much of a "normal" political party Forza Italia became, despite the personality of its leader and the relationship the latter entertained, for a while at least, with Italians. This is unusual: most populist leaders, or proto-populist leaders struggle to establish a party that functions autonomously from them; typically, they are torn between the necessary professionalization and the need to remain a movement that can claim non-professionalization and a more authentic link to the people. Not so in the case of Berlusconi. There are three reasons for this: one is that, as we noted earlier, Forza Italia met with electoral success so rapidly that there was little time for hesitation. The other is that, because of its meteoric rise, there were no factions in the party when it came to power: no ready-made groups that could internally disagree. And finally, as indicated earlier, despite this meteoric rise and the centrality of Berlusconi, many of its key political personnel came from the disbanded mainstream-right parties: they had experience. So, as noted by a number of authors, Forza Italia has in some ways been more like a conventional political party, within which "anti-political populism is entirely delegated to the leader, who has made it a trademark of his political style, but not a source of ideological inspiration" (Tarchi 2008: 86; Ruzza & Fella 2011: 166).

Shamelessness and pantomime

But in the meantime, Berlusconi refashioned Italian politics in two ways. First, he brought a new kind of "warts-and-all" persona to the heart of the public sphere, whereas previous corrupt politicians spent a lot of money and energy dissimulating it. This is not an argument about the debasement of politics or the decline in civility (although it seems there is plenty of room for those too!), but rather, an argument about what Italian citizens were moving toward with Berlusconi. Italians were not dupes about the level of corruption in their system, but Berlusconi's attitude (toward business, toward politics, toward sex) ushered in a new openness about it. This was the realization of a different kind of ordinariness – shamelessness – that tried to defend itself, but with a bit of a shrug. One, in other words, that had a "catch me if you can" kind of quality that sent out a message about what kind of behaviour was tolerable and expected. And the lengths to which Berlusconi was naturally willing to go, which for some conclusively demonstrated that he was pandering to no one.

Detractors, whatever their political home, and they were mainly on the left, were immediately accused of puritanism, of lacking a sense of humour and, in fact, of dishonesty – we're all in this corrupt system, so how can you preach? There is something very specific to Italian political life which is a combination of incredible lucidity and wantonness. Italians know who they are, but for a long time did not seem to think that they deserved any better. It is still unclear whether they do now. It is worth revisiting here the role of shame because it explains the infernal cycle in which Italian politics seem trapped and the sense of an unstoppable escalation. What kind of toll does a politics based on one bad choice, one bad bargain after another take on its citizens? This is well beyond partisan lines: you do not win one year and lose the next; everyone feels as though they are losing all the time, and that that they have helped to elect those who inflict the damage. This is one of the key questions in Italian politics, but it also sheds some light on some of the deeper springs of populism. A background of acquiescences (first in the context of the North–South question, then in the context of fascism – whose legacy was never properly examined or even taken quite seriously), followed by a complicit attitude toward corruption, nepotism, clientelism from one election to another with only brief respite, is the backdrop against which so much of the Italian populism we see today is articulated. This is not at all a castigation of individual Italians, but rather an exhortation to think of populism as a compulsion to get over the shame of one bad deal, by signing up to another one. Populism with its promises and disruption is also about distraction.

Berlusconi fought the charges against him and protested his innocence, but he just as often turned around and gave the verbal equivalent of a wink. All the while burying his opposition and his accusers in legal defence papers and leading them on wild-goose chases. And, of course, bemoaning the role of "politicized judges" who spent too much time getting in the way of politics. The question of whether anyone was duped by Berlusconi, rather than just gave in to him as a matter of expediency and as a lesser evil is worth posing (though difficult to answer).

The second way in which Berlusconi reshaped Italian politics was that his behaviour radicalized many of his opponents. By the time Beppe Grillo emerges with his Five Star Movement, those who were not in favour of Berlusconi were ready for just about anything else. Grillo takes Berlusconi's authenticity one step further: he storms the internet, promises revolution and flashes two fingers up at the political class. Gianni Riotta puts it best:

At this point, the polarization between the Berlusconi right and the anti-Berlusconi left created a situation in which no moderate, from any camp, could take the stage. [...] Politics was reduced to an exchange of scathing remarks on TV shows, with not a shred of reasoning to contribute to any proposals; this attitude infected the newspapers who took each other on like gladiators, from pro- or anti- Berlusconi camps [...] (Riotta 2013: 595)

Riotta's reference to gladiators echoes my own analysis of "colosseum politics", applied to many other contexts (in particular those taken with calling for referendums) (Fieschi 2017; Fieschi n.d.). There is no overstating the parlous state of the Italian political conversation at the time. When moderate Romano Prodi was elected in 2006, his failure was to be expected. No moderate, as Riotta points out, could have survived the climate of verbal violence, threats and gossip: Prodi was forced to resign in 2008. When Italians went back to the ballot-box they returned Berlusconi to power in a gesture that sealed the pantomime quality of Italian politics (rather than deal with the shame of complicity, Italians stared it down through the ballot box). Mired in the economic crisis which hit Italy almost as hard as it hit Greece, the debate was reduced to Berlusconi "yes" or "no".

The Lega and Beppe Grillo's Five Star Movement (M5S) made the most of it, only this time in a fully developed digital culture. Thus began, in earnest, Italy's age of populism. The year 2008 marks the beginning of populism's full ideological development in Italy: M5S began to capitalize on the deep transformation of the voters through its use of the Web, and the promise of a different, transparent and authentic bottom-up movement; while the Lega began to transcend its geographical limits and move southward with the aim of conquering Berlusconi strongholds through a discourse of common sense in the face of Italy's main challenges (chief amongst them immigration).

Out-populizing the populists? M5S and the rise of "vaffanculismo"

Italy is the home of neologisms: where the Germans pile on more words, Italians take one and give it an "ism". Beppe Grillo, the founder of M5S, created a famous one: he upped the ante from the already established *"menefreghismo"* ("I-do not-give-a-damnism"), to the definitely cruder "vaffanculismo" ("fuck-offism"). The expression is a good starting point for the style of M5S, what it has since struggled against, but above all the levels of frustration and fluidity it captured in the Italian electorate at that particular moment.

Online and offline

M5S has had a startling trajectory. It began its emergence in 2005 as a result of the encounter of the comedian Beppe Grillo and Gianroberto Casaleggio, a web consultant. They were an unlikely pair: Grillo, stout and chubby with a huge mass of curls that bop around as he gets excited (and he gets excited often); Casaleggio (who died in 2016) tall and pale, looked like something out of Rocky Horror. Grillo is fond of saying that when Casaleggio approached him to start a completely different type of movement around a blog – thereby bypassing Berlusconi's empire entirely – he thought he was crazy. But Casaleggio insisted that no one controlled the net, not even Berlusconi. And so www.beppegrillo.it was launched. It became Italy's most popular blog and the Movement spent its first few years developing a radically different platform. Two things are crucial about this foundational moment. The first is that the movement was at pains to point out that it was not a party. Indeed, a read of its statutes confirms this: the M5S "is not a political party nor is it intended to become one in the future", it gives "the totality of the users of the internet the role of government and leadership which is normally attributed to a few". It was also stated that the movement's symbol "is registered on behalf of Beppe Grillo, the sole owner of the rights to use it" (Art. 3).[4] As noted by Filippo Tronconi (2018), a claim that was pure rhetoric, given that at the very same time, M5S was fielding activists and, more to the point, candidates.[5]

---

4. See www.movimento5stelle.it (accessed 22 March 2019).
5. It is also worth noting that when Casaleggio died Grillo immediately appointed a five-person directorate (that included the movement's current leader and Deputy prime minister, Luigi Di Maio). Six months later, in October of 2016, Grillo dissolved the directorate and appointed himself sole leader of the movement. Davide Casaleggio, Gian-Roberto's son is heavily involved, as is Enrico Grillo,

The second important point is that it immediately asserted itself *both* online and offline. This duality would be reflected in everything it did. Offline, Beppe Grillo continued to host his stand-up comedy shows, and began to host his famous "Vaffanculo rallies", through which he recruited activists and developed networks on the ground. The Vaffanculo rallies[6] and the "Vaffa days", were held in more than 200 piazzas between 2007 and 2013. They tended to revolve around the projection onto a screen of the names of Italian politicians (and organizations) accused of corruption: and as Grillo listed the names and their alleged illicit activities, he yelled "vaffanculo" after each one to a crowd of thousands, who responded with a collective roar of "vafancullo" and a V-shaped gesture.[7] Grillo harangued the crowd, screamed his lungs out about corruption, capitalism, the environment, and used every available expletive against every corner of the Italian establishment (businesses, media, government, banks) who were ruining Italy and bleeding Italians dry. It was in one of these gatherings, in Bologna, that Grillo announced his key parliamentary initiatives: no parliamentary candidates with criminal records (which also ruled him out having a conviction for manslaughter in a car accident in which he was the driver in 1981), term limits of two legislatures for any representative, and a new electoral system based on direct preferences of the electorate (Agnew & Shin 2016). Over the course of that Vaffanculo rally in Bologna (in September 2007), he gathered 350,000 signatures in support of his initiative. Between his blog and his www.meetup.com website, Grillo mobilized 2 million people.

Online, Grillo seemed to practice what he preached: the blog became central to M5S and received critical acclaim from the likes of *The Observer*, *Forbes*, and *Time* magazine (Bordignon & Ceccarini 2013).

Beppe's nephew. The actual organigramme of the movement, not to mention the details of its financial affairs are the subject of complete opacity and much speculation. They have given rise to several investigations that invariable go nowhere as the main protagonists seem to be relatively uninformed as to the legal framework of the structure of which they are a part. Grillo, in other words keeps an extremely tight leash on information and the party has been increasingly accused of betraying its civic and popular roots.

6. There are plenty of clips on the M5sParlamento YouTube channel: https://www.youtube.com/user/M5SParlamento (accessed 22 March 2019).

7. "Beppe's Inferno", *The New Yorker*, 4 February 2008; available at: https://www.newyorker.com/magazine/2008/02/04/beppes-inferno (accessed 14 September 2018).

It became the place where Grillo typically outlined his views about the direction of the party and the policy positions that it should be adopting. Proposals were then voted on by party members through an online platform, "Rousseau" (previously M5OS), on a one-member-one-vote system. From 2013, when the party got into parliament, members were also invited to observe the party's livestreamed meetings in parliament, on the M5SParlamento YouTube channel. Above all, the party promised total transparency, complete access and unadulterated democracy. From the streaming of parliamentary debates, to the filming and recording of discussions with other politicians, to the manner in which preferences and votes were logged online, to the candidate selection process.

The honesty market?

What cannot be overestimated in the case of M5S is both the extent to which the objective was to upend politics entirely (via the use of the internet), and the transformation that was occurring in the Italian citizenry as a result of the growth of access to digital. In the case of M5S, this was made clear by Grillo from the very beginning. Playing on his own historical (self-proclaimed) status as a political outsider, Grillo's objective was to renew the Italian political class and revive Italian democracy from the bottom up and through radically new methods: "This is already a revolution. It has already started. You can't stop it anymore. I did not want it. It is not mine. It is the internet that changes: the internet is not just a language, it modifies relationships, the way we look at the world". As a result, he added, "We want to govern, but we do not want to simply change the power by replacing it with our own. We want a change of civilization, a change of world vision."[8]

Furthermore, Grillo argued: "We want to destroy everything, not rebuild on the same rubble. We have different ideas. You have to have a clean slate." And just in case we weren't clear: "The political parties are dead. Citizens need to detach themselves from the dead while they still can. [...] Politics is long since dead. Only vultures remain, who divide up the body of Italy. [...] and we are like David and Goliath. We only

---

8. BBC interview, 28 February 2013; available at: http://www.bbc.co.uk/news/world-europe-21613939 (accessed 22 March 2019).

have the Web, the MeetUps, our enthusiasm and my meetings. They have all the rest."[9]

In some respects, this message has been extraordinarily effective:[10] In the regional elections of 2010, M5S scored 7 per cent, but the electoral breakthrough came in the 2012 local elections, when M5S won the wealthy city of Parma in the North, as well as a couple of smaller towns together with 10 per cent of the vote. Six short years later, M5S fielded candidates across Italy (selecting them, more or less transparently, via their online tools) and scored an impressive 25.5 per cent of the vote for the Chamber of Deputies and 24 per cent for the Senate; M5S stormed the institutions and became Italy's largest party overnight. Kept out of power by a game of alliances, M5S were a ferocious opposition. Like Mélenchon's deputies they chose to break with Italian convention and "dress down" in jeans and sneakers. Unlike Mélenchon's party they secured power through a mix of tough-talking and hard work (of the 109 deputies, none had held political office before). Most noteworthy, the "*Grillini*", as activists are known, continued their MeetUps and remained connected to the grassroots. It is estimated that tens of thousands of them devoted several evenings a month to the MeetUps. In the 2018 general elections M5S gained 32 per cent of the vote – again it was the biggest party in Italy –and as I write, it has been in a coalition government with the Lega since June 2018.

In terms of themes, M5S is the same sort of mix as Mélenchon's FI. The common populist tropes are there: the people, the betrayal by the elite (with a strong emphasis on obvious corruption), the nation as something to be protected (Grillo, for example, was critical of large-scale immigration) and above all, authenticity. As for the themes, they are those of the radical left: nationalization, flat tax, versions of a universal basic income. With a heavy dash of digital.

Grillo and Casaleggio created a party that brought together all of the key concepts of populism, but it did so with devastatingly effective digital means. Such means, as pointed out by Grillo, are about much more than internet use: they have the power to transform people, their

---

9. Cited in Bordignon & Ceccarini 2013.
10. It is worth mentioning that a lot of this rhetoric of building from the rubble of the "old" civilization is very reminiscent of fascist texts, including Julius Evola's foundational *Men Among the Ruins*.

relationship to each other, and to politics. It is the combination of the Rousseau platform and the use of MeetUp *with* a promise of direct democracy:

> It should be the citizens and the local community who govern cities through the Internet, using collective intelligence. The web is revolutionizing the relationship between citizens and institutions making direct democracy feasible, as applied in ancient Greece [...]. From our side, we want to give the tools to the citizens. We have an operating system called Rousseau, to which every Italian citizen can subscribe for free. There they can vote in regional and local elections and check what their local MPs are proposing. Absolutely any citizen can even suggest laws in their own name. This is something never before directly seen in democracy and neither Tsipras nor Podemos have done it.[11]

And with a promise of transparency:

> It is a tremendous revolution, when our people come in, there will be no more theft, no more stealing, honesty will come back into fashion. He's honest? Okay, come over. He steals? No. Shut up. Steal. Honest? OK. The market of honesty. The honesty market. OK? This is a dream. The movement is a dream of what could happen in 20 or 30 years. Not now. Now, nothing will happen.[12]

And with the traditional core concepts of populism, for example, the conspiracy and amateurism of experts:

> It is their strength to make us not understand, we are here to understand, to simplify, to bring out and to say, "gentlemen, this Europe is not the one we want" [...] These people are

---

11. "Five Star Movement plans to 'revolutionize democracy' through online voting and e-petitions", *The Local*, 5 April 2017; available at: https://www.thelocal.it/20170405/five-star-movement-plans-democracy-revolution (accessed 9 September 2017).

12. Beppe Grillo, BBC interview, 28 February 2013; available at: http://www.bbc.co.uk/news/world-europe-21613939 (accessed 22 March 2019).

amateurish and then they have this attitude to favour crime, because with their rule they have changed treaties, treaties signed by fine gentlemen [...] But if I say that on television, then big economists say a clown is saying these things, I am the clown. I haven't any qualifications in merit. They have all the Bocconi's professors, big economists. They haven't ever hit the nail on the head. In 20 years, nobody has foreseen 2008's crisis.[13]

And the appeal to common sense and the bypassing of complexity, such as Grillo's suggestion in June 2018 that members of the Senate be elected by sortition, rather than have parties select their candidates for office.[14] This is typical of Grillo's response to complex policy issues. The same can be said of his proposals to democratize day-to-day decision making through a system of online consultations and public petitions. The simplicity and communicability of the proposed solutions – regardless of feasibility – make them ideal for diffusion on social media whilst also contributing to Grillo's image as a common-sense, straight-talker.

The key point here is that the promise of immediacy, transparency and seamlessness that characterizes the digital medium and is embedded in populist promises is not just evoked, it is put into practice through the tools proposed by M5S.

Politics as mirror: vote for you!

Over time what emerged with M5S, facilitated by the currency of digital trust and the promise of immediacy and transparency, is politics as mirror: a political movement whose key aim was to sell real democracy, the best democracy, as a vote for yourself. Indeed, one of the 2012 posters for elections in Sicily read "*Votate per voi*" (Vote for you). In fact, a survey of M5S supporters found that 76 per cent trust the internet as a source, compared to 11 per cent who trust the press (34% among the

---

13. Grillo speaking at European Parliament in Strasbourg, July 2014; available at https://www.youtube.com/watch?v=KnthcaB1-CA (accessed 22 March 2019).
14. "Il 'sortition' di Grillo e gli statisti per caso", *Il Foglio*, 29 June 2018; available at: https://www.ilfoglio.it/politica/2018/06/29/news/il-sortition-di-grillo-e-gli-statisti-per-caso-203032/ (accessed 10 September 2018).

wider population), and less than 4 per cent who trust television (40% among Italians overall) (Bartlett *et al.* 2012). Whether these attitudes predate Grillo's scathing attacks on the media, or whether he is the reason they feel this way, is not clear. But what is clear is that, while Grillo was obviously able to exploit the consequences of and the resentment generated by the economic crisis, he was also able to create a movement based on a different expectation of politics. One that essentially bypasses representation in favour of what some have termed "representativeness": the demand to be represented by yourself as the only authentic voice capable of doing so.

The pressures of power

Rapid accession to power in combination with the selection of candidates with no political experience took their toll on M5S. Their mayors (in particular in Rome) were a disaster, and the inexperience, as well as the rather chequered background, of many of their MPs led to extraordinary behaviour in the chamber (a chamber that has seen some pretty extraordinary behaviour). As a result, in the run up to the elections of 2018, two things happened. The first was a decision to field more credible candidates. Not necessarily people with political experience, but people with credible professional backgrounds. The second important measure was the replacement of Beppe Grillo as leader by the ambitious, young but relatively unknown Luigi Di Maio, who emerged through the party's tried and tested digital platforms, although potentially not without a little extra help from the webmaster.

Despite Grillo's assertion that his new party runs an unmediated form of direct democracy, he has frequently been criticized for appearing to intervene in ways that contradict the party's own rules and ethos. The party's MPs have complained, sometimes publicly, that there is little freedom of conscience. They are expected to behave as mouthpieces of the leadership rather than representatives of its members, or face expulsion from the party, which is usually preceded by an "excommunication" on Grillo's blog (Bordignon & Ceccarini 2015). This method has been used extensively: "By mid-2017, the expelled parliamentarians, by means of a post on the blog, numbered 40 (21 deputies – 19% of the parliamentary group – and 19 senators – 35% of the group), a clear indicator that internal pluralism is hardly tolerated" (Tronconi 2018). Grillo's blogposts seem to change depending on their content, but they take on various roles, from personal position papers to something closer to party diktats: this is not about direct participation, this is about passing down orders. This shows no sign of abating under the party's new leader, Luigi Di Maio who is both Italy's deputy prime minister and minister for the economy in coalition with the Lega.

After Grillo? Not quite

Di Maio is a much less flamboyant character whose relative obscurity probably served the party well in the run up to the 2018 elections. Grillo supposedly disappeared from sight, although he continues to run his blog and is extremely active in the background. Di Maio's presence contributed to "normalizing" and depersonalizing the party slightly – something which it needed to do. And something that did not strike its members as odd given the premium placed on the potential rise of ordinary people. Many argue that Di Maio's youth and lack of experience also make him far more pliable to the leadership. Di Maio also represents continuity with the party's rather ambiguous ideological line: ambiguous on Europe, on immigration, but also on its placement on the left–right spectrum. Grillo was skilled at purposefully scrambling the lines, in part to remain as catch-all as possible, in part because he truly believes the process he is offering is the ideology: bottom up, from scratch and largely virtual. While Di Maio is also centrist in his approach to politics, there is a much more left of centre wing, represented by Alessandro di Battista, which advocates that the party should anchor itself firmly on the left, and above all, remain a movement rather than an ordinary party of government. The sparring went on between Di Maio and Di Battista until the results of the March 2018 elections. At which point entering into a coalition government with the Lega's Matteo Salvini – and therefore likely to have to compromise on some of the party's key policies – the party clearly signalled a centrist approach. Di Battista left Italy for a long South America road-trip. Although by late 2018, he had already, in typical M5S manner, announced his "virtual" return on a number of the movement's platforms.

In his incarnation as minister for the economy, joint deputy PM, and co-leader of the coalition (a coalition that almost did not see the light of day given the strangeness of the bedfellows), Di Maio has been very much relegated to junior partner. The results of the election gave M5S 32 per cent of the vote, and the Lega 17.5 per cent. However, in the space of only a few months Salvini was able to impose himself as the dominant partner, and raise his popular support to equal that of M5S and even, on occasion surpass it. The return therefore of a stronger, less procedurally acceptable but more politically astute leader is not to be ruled out.

Berlusconi ushered a new form of politics based around a different kind of authenticity: one that was not above raising a mirror to people's worst fears and cynicism and anchored in blatant, or authentic, lying; M5S ran with it and added a fully digital offer of immediacy and direct-ness in an attempt to circumvent the conspiracy of institutional politics. The Lega has developed something in parallel which draws heavily on conspiracy theories – conspiracies by central government, by Europe and by the banks – and a very immediate relationship to politics via Matteo Salvini; Above all the Lega proposes a revolution of common sense by "taking Italians seriously".

The Lega and the triumph of common-sense "chat"

The Lega has had a remarkable trajectory since it first came to promi-nence in the 1980s. Initially founded as the Lega Lombarda before form-ing alliances with other northern and central Italian regionalist parties, including the Liga Veneta and Piemont Autonomista, it became known as the Lega Nord from 1991 under the leadership of Umberto Bossi. From its origins as a disparate series of small regionalist movements and parties, it briefly became a party of government from 1994 and served in the Berlusconi cabinets of the 2000s. In 2018, the new leader Matteo Salvini, immediately rebranded the party as the Lega to broaden its appeal beyond its northern electoral base. In the 2018 general elec-tions the party received 17 per cent of the vote (including votes from the South) and after forming a coalition with M5S, it became the junior party – but the dominant voice – in the national government. In a few short years the Lega had managed to become a national party in a way that it had never done before. And to refashion Italian populism around its promise of disruption and authentic Italianness.

The Lega began building momentum during the 1980s. The actions of the DC and its successive governments paved the way for its rise. The

DC relied heavily on clientelism to shore up its interests in the South, requiring high and growing levels of public expenditure, financed from tax revenues provided mainly by the wealthier North. This allowed the Lega to argue that the tax-and-spending activities of the so-called *partitocrazia* were regionally biased against the North (Newell 2010). One of its early slogans was *"Roma ladrona"* ("thieving Rome"), implying that responsibility for policy that disadvantaged the North lay with national representatives in the capital. The slogan successfully encapsulated the Lega's anti-state and anti-politics sentiments and combined them with its regionalist outlook.

The party was founded on an understanding of the people as both "ethnos" and "demos" (Tarchi 2008: 85–6). It purported to represent the interests of the people of northern Italy over those of the South, as well those of the people against the elite. But the dichotomy, especially now, extends beyond national borders by pitting a homogenous Italian community against the migrant outsider, that threaten its wealth and security. The Lega had also occasionally taken issue with the European Union as an external source of frustration.

Under Salvini, populist ideas have come home to roost. The common sense of Italians is regularly pitted against the incomprehensible bureaucracy of the EU (given its status as a party of government, the Lega had to switch from blaming Rome, to blaming the EU more exclusively), and in fact, the main promise is two-fold: "a common-sense revolution"[15] and "Italians First", two expressions that are both plastered on the campaign bus and serve to christen most rallies.

Much of the rhetoric is designed to be as blunt as possible – no *politichese*. It is interesting because in contrast to Grillo and the Five Star Movement, this party prides itself on decency. It is looking to severely disrupt the status quo, but is never vulgar, and very seldom funny. This is not just because Salvini is not a comedian, but because the aim is precisely not to be on a stage; it is to be much closer to his voters and to all Italians. To be in conversation with them.

His promise is to save the grand gestures, for officials; hence his picking a fight with Europe, with those who he claims have both betrayed and belittled Italy and Italians. The disjunction between the friendly,

---

15. See https://www.leganord.org/la-rivoluzione-del-buonsenso (accessed 22 March 2019).

common-sense chat to camera reserved not just for his supporters but for all Italians (such as when he appears on talk shows: relaxed, fluent and good-humoured) and his aggressive tone when speaking to and about foreign leaders is effective in displaying his authentic love of Italians, and what he is willing to do for them. His aim is to take the disruption right into enemy territory.

Salvini mobilized anti-EU discourse throughout the 2018 election campaign, promising to ignore EU spending limits and hold a referendum on Italy's membership of the eurozone. He then renounced the latter proposal but has continued his war of words with and against Brussels, and against all its supporters (chief amongst them French President Macron). When the Morandi bridge in Genoa partially collapsed, killing 43 people in August 2018, Salvini blamed the incident on the EU's spending limits and its consequences for infrastructure spending. The preparations for the European Parliament elections of May 2019 were one of the high-water marks of confrontation and disruption as Salvini seized the challenge raised by President Macron and squarely positioned himself as Macron's main European adversary: the fight over Europe's true nature would be between him (as the defender of a Europe of peoples and sovereign states), and Macron as the defender of the status quo and a Europe of elites and free movement (as Salvini has often said "the EU does not want free movement, it wants slaves. Well Italy is no longer going to act as a trade route").

Whilst it is the case that many of the Lega's current positions are long-standing, its style and methods of communications have changed significantly, as has the emphasis and scope of its policies. When Salvini took over, the party began its transformation from a regional to a national force: a few days after his election he publicly apologized for his frequent attacks on southern Italy and its inhabitants. The party's primary aims of regional autonomy were dropped and party policy shifted to more typical populist themes, including immigration, law and order and identity as well as recurrent attacks on the EU. Underpinning all of these is the typical core ideas of the supremacy of the people's common sense as well as those of the betrayal inflicted by the opposition (the elites Salvini must continue to point to, lest someone pick up that he is now, "them").

Most political leaders take to social media regularly, however Salvini, much like Grillo did in M5S, creates an intense and almost intimate relationship with his supporters. While M5S was focused on creating networks of angry and frustrated citizens and broadcasting Grillo's views and pronouncements, Salvini set the stage for a personal relationship with every citizen. In 2014, Salvini went as far as to pose wearing next to nothing, under a duvet for *Oggi* magazine.[16] The pictures were auctioned for charity on eBay. A recent study of the Lega's Facebook presence found that it was the relationship between the party leader and his supporters that was the most significant factor in likeability of online posts. His involvement was more important than any other variable in explaining the popularity of a message among Lega fans (Bobba 2018). It is also worth noting that Salvini has continued to make progress in a wide geographical area: making headway in central Italian regions that had previously been dominated by the left, and even in the South.

This direct connection with (potential) supporters enables Salvini to reassert both his own political perspective, and bolster support for his programme amongst his followers. These controversial interjections work in his favour on several levels as can be seen in a Facebook post from August 2018:

> A 25-year-old girl was attacked in the Milan train station, saving herself from RAPE only through use of pepper spray. The rapist was arrested today, let's hope this time he finds a judge who keeps him in prison for YEARS. P.S. I am not allowed to tell you that the rapist is Nigerian, an illegal immigrant with a criminal record, or I will be accused of RACISM.[17]

This post is exemplary of the Lega and Salvini's central themes that are prominent on the Lega's agenda, including law and order, identity, and immigration, which are used to legitimize his well-known views on these issues. Like most populist parties of the right it mobilizes an "us/them" distinction by suggesting that "illegal immigrants" are de facto criminals, whilst Italians are victims (he failed to mention that the victim of this crime was an immigrant herself). It also alludes to a broken system of Italian justice which is characterized as a lottery.

---

16. See http://www.milanotoday.it/politica/foto-salvini-nudo-ebay-asta-beneficenza.html (accessed 22 March 2019).
17. Matteo Salvini, on Facebook, 3 August 2018.

But perhaps even more importantly, it is the tone and nature of expression that catch our attention: the use of Trump-like capitalization suggests informality, and expression that is spontaneous, unguarded, informal ("let's hope that this time he finds a judge who keeps him in prison for YEARS"), whilst also offering his own immediate extrajudicial verdict on the case that complements his hard-line stances on crime and immigration. It also mobilizes the anti-judicial, anti-elite sentiments that frequently appeared in Berlusconi's political discourse throughout the 2000s. Finally, it immediately points the finger at the potential accusations he knows he will get in return. The effect is to neutralize any such accusations: "you are so predictable, so scripted, so unable to think for yourself, so fake, that I already know what you're about to accuse me of", the message seems to say.

Most importantly, Salvini seems always available, always accessible. There is none of the traditional gate-keepers who might distort the message or get in the way of the relationship. And while this is definitely reminiscent of Trump, Salvini knows the value of his virtual presence: the live Facebook posts, accessible anywhere, anytime, that broadcast him close-up and personal, go well beyond a stream of Tweets. They build a relationship, they build trust in his authenticity as both a leader and an ordinary Italian, doing his best to connect with you, and doing his job. This deluge of posts allows Salvini to appear as though he is responding to events, whilst constantly (re)asserting policy positions and his own outlook beyond the confines of less accessible, infrequently published manifestos.[18]

The fact that he often speaks to camera while holding his phone is another extremely useful tactic in this competition for authenticity. As the messages are filmed "on the go", there can be no accusation of staging. The message is that this is not a performance, this is someone who is partly reporting (look what I have found out for you), partly sharing thoughts (I can't wait to tell you), and partly connecting as you would with someone you have a daily relationship with (in their regularity and tone, many of his live posts are not far off the daily "check-in" phone call to mamma). There is a familiarity that is one that is both friendship but

---

18. The sheer volume of posts is also noteworthy: in 2015 whilst his online following was considerably lower (c.400,000) than it was during the 2018 election (2.9 million), he posted on average ten times per day (Stille 2018).

also family. But there is also an intimation of directness and truth. One clip summarizes his aims quite well. Available on his Salvini Official Facebook page, it captures Salvini filming himself in front of a house that serves as accommodation for migrants. Salvini serves a running commentary: "You will not catch any mainstream channels showing you this stuff. They say they're running from war but look" – he zooms in on the open door – "they're all watching football on TV inside". He yells out: "does anyone speak Italian here? […] no of course not. Why would they try and speak Italian? Look, they're all going inside. They must be tired because they're running from war" (uses air quotes here).[19]

The clip is extremely effective: it conveys Salvini's main message, namely that he wants to show you what everyone else is trying to hide from you. And he's doing it himself, he's not sending someone, or trusting the mainstream media to report on this. If you want something done ask him. And the commentary is laconic: it is not terribly descriptive, it lets the images do the talking, with just enough comment to raise suspicion. There are dozens of such clips (interspersed with the requisite kissing of babies clips).

Prior to the 2018 election, he frequently appeared in public dressed informally; often wearing t-shirts emblazoned with the Lega logo, and the name of the place he was visiting on the campaign trail. It made him look like a fan of both the place where he was and of himself, like someone on tour with his band. When such images were reproduced in the media, it amplified the new geographical aims of the party, he was everywhere, and he was on the move. Energetic and less stuffy: just stepping off a train, just about to get on stage, just grabbing a bite, just driving. It allowed Salvini to appear active, unstoppable in fact, as though he really meant it. During the drawn out negotiations between the elections of March 2018 and the formation of the coalition government with M5S, the clothes were designed to highlight the distinction between the realm of his supporters (to whom he continued to send small clips while wearing a T-shirt) and his capacity to weather the charade of established politics when it was necessary and wear a suit. The fact that the tie was often undone suggested (not unlike Obama's rolled up sleeves) that he was hard at work but also looked suspiciously like the noose of formal politics had been loosened.

---

19. See Matteo Salvini's 2018 campaign video, Facebook, February 2018.

Italy, no matter what the tensions between the two populist coalition partners, has offered the world a sobering message: populists from across the party spectrum can cooperate for a while – which suggests their populism is more important than their partisan differences (much as populism always claims). It has also offered one of the most striking displays of populist evolution and of the intrinsic link between populism's core ideas and the political culture fostered by digital and its fantasy of radical transparency. Regardless of the fate of the coalition Italy, like many developed democracies is engaging in a political experiment that while intrinsically Italian, suggests that it will have changed the parameters of politics and the expectations of citizens. More disappointment no doubt follows. What will this experiment lead to next, now that populism is even more firmly on the Italian agenda?

6

The UK and the absolute populist fantasy: taking back control

On 16 June 2016, a week before the date of the UK's referendum on the European Union, my phone suddenly flashed with several breaking news alerts: it was early afternoon and the shocking news was that Jo Cox, the young and brilliant MP for Batley and Spen had been shot dead by a man who, according to witnesses, had yelled "This is for Britain!", "Keep Britain independent!" and "Put Britain first!" A week later, like many others, I made my way to Trafalgar Square for a memorial in her honour. I had a broken ankle and stood well to the side on my crutches. At one point we were asked to join hands, which felt like a very un-British thing to do and somewhat perilous in my case. But the man next to me extended his hand with a smile and so there we were: me wobbly on one crutch, and him providing balance. Although the fabric of the nation had already been frayed by the campaign, and by Jo Cox's murder, there was at that moment a desire to overcome the divisions that had been made so deep and so glaring by a referendum campaign that had been ugly and brutal – to the point of unleashing murder. It would also really be the last time in which a public conversation took place about the fact that a young MP, a mother of two, was murdered in broad daylight during the referendum campaign. While her name comes up, as it is both fondly remembered and attached to a number of causes, there has been no discussion about it; political violence has been swept under the carpet by blaming the murderer's mental illness. Yet one wonders whether the acrimony between the two sides (Leave and Remain), the still-born deals, the miscommunication, the sense of a great unravelling of British politics and a shaming of its political land-scape for ego, greed, and incompetence can really be entirely discon-nected from the death that marked the campaign's lowest point.

I am putting the finishing touches to this chapter as the negotiations of the UK's withdrawal from the European Union enter their final stage.

As final stages go, it is quite spectacular: several years of negotiations have produced more division, more rancour both across and within parties, as well as within the country, than the referendum campaign itself. The toll feels particularly dramatic for several reasons. In part because the decision to leave the EU feels far more irreversible than an election result: in democracies, election results, if truly disastrous, can generally be remedied a few years later. The referendum decision, even though reversibility is theoretically possible, feels more permanent – in part because the period since the result and the triggering of Article 50 (the legal mechanism by which the UK signalled its intention to withdraw from the EU) has been at least as polarizing as the campaign. But the sense of irreversibility is not only linked to the result, but rather to two other things. The first is that what has been seen, cannot be unseen: what has been revealed about the UK to the UK, cannot be hidden again. We have seen who we are, or at least an aspect of who we are that had been kept hidden, buried or ignored for generations. It is the revelations of the referendum that, for both supporters of Leave and supporters of Remain are barely bearable. That they have been living side by side with strangers, that they have been misunderstood by their fellow citizens, that they inhabit different worlds, different emotional spheres. And this is exacerbated by the speed with which this seems to have happened. Between 2012, when the UK hosted the world for the Olympics and staged an opening ceremony that managed to pull off that most British of things – tongue in cheek pride complete with a parachuting sovereign and dancing NHS nurses – and today, only a few short years have gone by. In comparison to the long tail of populism in France and Italy, UK populists look to have been remarkably successful in a very short span of time. What happened?[1]

The great European exception?

It is worth remembering that for a long time received wisdom held that the UK was immune to populism: it was the great European exception. While everywhere else in Europe – from the 1980s onwards – electorates

---

1. Jonathan Coe's novel *Middle England* is a poignant account of this traumatic political drift.

seemed increasingly inclined to turn to populist options (especially on the right), the UK electorate seemed intent on bucking the trend and this was taken as axiomatic of British political life. The UK would not go the way of the continental populist domino effect. This is what "excitable continentals" did, not Brits. Perhaps this was due to the continued – psychological and rhetorical – dominance of the Second World War moment in which Britain appeared unscathed and resisting. But the fact is that the slow and steady development of populism in the UK went almost undetected until the creation of UKIP, and possibly until the Brexit vote itself. A number of commentators sounded the alarm around a very different form of rebellion, the far-right British National Party (BNP) and its meagre gains in the early noughties, but few, if any, voices identified the populist UKIP as the real danger. The fact that tabloids had been busy developing a terrain for populist argumentation – through the conflation of immigration, loss of sovereignty and the European Union, in an atmosphere of growing distrust vis-à-vis parties and politicians – did not register because it was not being translated into party politics or votes (aside from declines in turn-out and increased volatility in voter choices). And then, all of a sudden, the Brexit story became the populist "success" story (if that is not an oxymoron).

Conservatism and populism

Thatcherism as proto-populism?

UKIP's populism, however, did have some precursors – and many would argue that Thatcherism was a foretaste of things to come. It is even arguable that the French FN/RN, and Margaret Thatcher's brand of Conservatism present some similarities: in their nationalism, in their disdain for established elites, in their appeals to common sense, and their hatred of the left. Indeed, so much so that both have been labelled "populist". What strikes me as particularly relevant across these two cases is, (1) their desire to call into question the postwar consensus and the legacy of the 1960s (economically, socially, culturally, but also the political legacy of decolonization); and most importantly (2) their willingness to carry this out by accusing all elites (especially the left, but also the mainstream right) of having betrayed the country and letting it go to hell in a hand-cart. Key to their appeal was the central claim that, elites – including those on their side of the political spectrum – who claimed to have the people and the nation's interest at heart, had in fact protected both their own liberal, and perhaps more cosmopolitan, interests first, as well as their narrow partisan interests. In the case of Thatcher, you could add recurring references to the permissive 1960s, the erosion of parental authority, and the ebbing of "British values" such as thrift and common sense.

In fact, by the mid-1970s, you could argue that Thatcher and Le Pen shared a diagnosis: that prosperity has led to weakness of will, that permissiveness has led to indolence and scrounging, that technocracy has led to bloating and mission-creep, and that the loss of empire had led to the nation's declining power and prestige on the international stage. This also heralded the emergence of a particular type of anti-immigrant rhetoric from both leaders, in which migrants were not just "scroungers", but individuals or groups that had taken advantage of the goodness of the nation and were undermining it from within (let's not forget that Enoch Powell's – often misquoted – "rivers of blood" speech had been delivered in 1968, a mere 11 years before Margaret Thatcher took office). Most importantly they both argued that all of this has happened under the watch, indeed with the active encouragement, of elites on both sides of the political divide (although each of them held the left in special contempt) who had gotten carried away with self-aggrandizing projects, and ignored the needs and demands of the people.

Neither Thatcher nor Le Pen spare the right (or, in her case, the Conservative Party); both believe that "their camp" has sold out: Le Pen despised de Gaulle once he became president, and Thatcher loathed the conciliatory, pro-Keynesian one-nation Toryism of the postwar era. And it is this disappointment in, and contempt for, their natural political home, that forged their particular brand of proto-populist spite. Both leaders rejected the consensus politics that the right has adopted. And in both cases, there was a longing to turn the clock back to a time before contemporary party politics.

Thatcher and authoritarian populism

For Thatcher, the lost, golden past and the height of British civilization from which the country had fallen was that of the (imagined and re-imagined) Victorians: an era of innovation in the service of national pride, of exuberant, liberal expansion in the form of empire, tempered by strict social mores and personal rectitude. Thatcherism was a puzzle: something was happening, and no one quite knew what to do with it, it escaped the rules of traditional left/right politics. It spoke unlike any traditional conservative politician, and it was a giant assault on the "acquis" (social and cultural) of the postwar years, and especially the 1960s. From the leadership of the Conservative Party, she seemed hell-bent on smashing the privileges of traditional elites (e.g. the civil service, universities), whilst at the same time appealing to timeless traditional (conservative with a small "c") values (thrift, common sense, godliness, respect).

The concept of "authoritarian populism" drew attention to Thatcherism's capacity to bring to the forefront of the political landscape the nostalgia felt by some for an order that was disappearing, a nationalism that had been banished by the postwar status quo, all the while laying the blame for all this not just on the door-step of the left, but also on the door-step of her own camp.

But Thatcher, while unorthodox in her tactics, subscribed to an organic vision of change: in other words a conservative vision. Much has been made of her criticism of compromise ("standing in the middle of the road is very dangerous; you get knocked down by traffic from both sides"), of the berating of certain Conservative Party members for being "wet", and of her strong-woman tactics. But it was never about revolution, it was about evolution and faith in a predictable order that has triumphed in the past and a plan to recapture it. It is in other words, a conservatism seeking to adapt to mass politics.

An opening for populism

Yet Thatcherism's flirtation with populism was nevertheless a form of Conservatism whose core concepts could easily accommodate a mutation into more fully developed populist ideology. And, as Tim Bale argues, from William Hague to Michael Howard, via Duncan Smith (in other words from 1997 to 2005), the Conservative Party developed a strong brand of populist Euroscepticism. This is particularly the case for William Hague (leader between 1997 and 2001) who strode into "unashamedly populist territory" (Bale 2016) resulting in a series of authoritarian and nativist interventions on law and order and immigration, culminating in the so-called "foreign land" speech of 2001 (Bale 2018: 266).

It is worth citing a few choice excerpts of Hague's speech[2]: they are a reminder both of how narrow the bridge between British Conservatism and populism has been since the 1980s, as well as a reminder that 2016 is not the abrupt turning point so many make it out to be. The sure signs that what would unfold under the banner of UKIP a decade or so after Hague (and certainly by 2016) was incubated in the Conservative Party early on. These are all of the ideas that we outlined earlier:

The claim to speak for a voiceless majority:

> But above all we're ready to speak for the people of Britain: for the mainstream majority who have no voice, for the hardworking people who feel they are ignored, for the men and women who despair that their country is being taken from them [...] A Conservative Government that speaks with the voice of the British people.

The appeals to instinct (rather than emotion):

> Well if there's one thing above all that sets me apart from Tony Blair, it is this: I'm not embarrassed to articulate the instincts of the British people!

The relentless invocation of common sense as what binds the people together:

> The governing of this country has drifted far away from the decent, plain speaking common sense of its people. It is time to bring it back. It is time to bring Britain home.

On education:

> Let's not be afraid to speak the common-sense truth: you cannot have high standards without good discipline. [...] Let's

---

2. Full speech is available at https://www.theguardian.com/politics/2001/mar/04/conservatives.speeches (accessed 22 March 2019).

trust the common-sense instinct that says that children need a structured day [...] People know that it is just common sense. And I trust the people.

The entire speech in fact is built on the claim that the then (Labour) government had nothing but disdain for the people:

> It seems common sense to you and me. But Labour, once again, prefers to listen to the self-appointed experts: to the liberal sociologists [...] We have a Government that has contempt for the views of the people it governs [...] There is nothing that the British people can talk about, that this Labour Government doesn't deride.

And to conclude, the promise of "a Conservative Government never embarrassed or ashamed of the British people".

The next leader, Michael Howard, pushed for a referendum on the EU constitutional treaty. This fusion of populist elements with a traditionally Eurosceptic tone, ended up strengthening a core of Euroscepticism – which, in fact, did nothing for the Conservative Party in the polls. When David Cameron was elected in 2006, he changed tack. In an attempt to modernize the party, he moved away from such rhetoric: "At a time when the massive influx of East Europeans into the United Kingdom occasioned by EU enlargement was beginning, and as rising concern about that influx began to fuse with anxiety among Eurosceptic voters and politicians about moves towards further integration, the Tories seemed to have their minds elsewhere" (Bale 2018 267).

According to Bale again, Cameron's change of tack and his embrace of a more liberal conservatism "created a space that UKIP could almost have been designed to fill, as long, that is, as it could find itself an entrepreneurial champion capable of seizing the opportunity and putting its case. In September 2006, it did just that by electing as its leader Nigel Farage" (*ibid.*: 267).

Looking at the ideological sequencing of these events is important: it suggests that UKIP's opportunity was handed to them by the Conservative Party's vacating of the populist stage; but, even more strikingly, that it was Conservative Party actions that allowed for a more fully developed populism to emerge with UKIP. So, Conservatism nurtured populism, then by retreating from it created an opening for it: enter UKIP.

The triumph of populism in the UK: UKIP

The United Kingdom Independence Party (UKIP) was initially founded as the Federalist League in 1991. Under a succession of leaders, it did not do particularly well (although it upped its membership when the well-known, ex-Labour MP, broadcaster Robert Kilroy-Silk was a member and an MEP) – until Farage took over in 2006. Farage had left the Conservative Party in 1992 in protest at the signing of the Maastricht Treaty. In many respects he was in line with previous UKIP leaders: sovereigntist and deeply Eurosceptic, his contempt for Brussels and the EU in evidence at every turn of phrase – the EU was a money-pit, a basket-case, stuffed with people "who had never done a proper job".

UKIP's rise and behaviour were not well-tracked in the run-up to the Brexit vote, or at least not until the European elections of 2014 and the general election of 2015 where their gains were significant enough to draw attention: in the local elections of 2013 UKIP captured 20 per cent of the vote, and 147 councillors (up from 9); and in 2014 the party essentially "won" the European elections by going from 16 per cent in the 2009 European elections to 27.4 per cent in 2014. By the time the General Election of 2015 came around UKIP was the UK's third largest party on 12.6 per cent of the national vote. One reason for this blind-spot was the overwhelming focus (in the UK and elsewhere) on the far right. Articles and headlines were devoted to the BNP, and then to the English Defence League, but few paid enough attention to UKIP before 2013 (see Fieschi 2005). By then, they were already in full swing.

But, aside from the opening created by the Conservative Party under Cameron, what might account for UKIP's success from 2013 onwards and, in particular, its capacity to deliver its core promise, namely a referendum on the European Union and a majority to leave? I will not focus on the internal politics of the Conservative Party and what drove David Cameron to call for a referendum on membership of the EU. Rather I want to explore how UKIP was able to capitalize on a set of dynamics and ideas present in the UK.

Making sense of the referendum

One of the best and most balanced accounts of the motivations behind the Brexit vote and the key developments that shaped the outcome is the volume by Geoffrey Evans and Anand Menon (2017). In it, the authors trace the convergence of the British two-party system as a result of "TINA" ("There Is No Alternative") politics: "An increasingly disenchanted electorate was thus confronted with a limited set of political choices. And this created a climate of rebellion" (Evans & Menon 2017: 45). But the authors also record and illustrate the change in values of the British electorate, the role of class (rather than simply immigration versus economics), and in particular the educational divide between those who voted Leave and those who voted Remain. In their volume a fuller picture appears of an electorate increasingly disillusioned, disenfranchised and deskilled. And thus, willing to vote for any alternative: from the politics of TINA to, what I have called elsewhere, the politics of "ABY" ("Anyone But You").

There are two striking things about the analyses of the results of the referendum. The first is the number of analyses that insist on viewing the vote in favour of leaving as result of *either* economic deprivation, or feelings of cultural exclusion. They are inextricably linked. Countering the economic explanation by arguing that some of the wealthier home counties voted to leave is missing the point about what constitutes the class culture of the home counties. Much as countering the cultural explanation with an argument about income levels is missing the point about what role income plays in people's lives and how it shapes outlooks and attitudes (see Counterpoint 2017). And it is precisely because of how these factors intersect and cross-cut party politics (much as they do in many European democracies) that the Conservative Party in the UK found itself compelled to call the referendum. More on this in a moment.

The much-vaunted accusation that Cameron called a referendum exclusively to address divisions in his own party", is designed to imply that Cameron's motives were shallow. Yes, he could not "put country over party", and yes, it was absolutely about partisanship. This partisanship, structured around a form of loyalty to the Conservative Party, is one that few people seem to measure nowadays and yet nothing about the run-up to the referendum, the campaign, or the negotiations since, can be understood if the nature and strength of this loyalty both from party members and above all from its politicians is not factored in.[3] But it was anything but shallow. The fact is that the Conservative Party (much as the Labour Party too) was simply no longer able to secrete a stance that could address the whole of its electorate, let alone insiders. While it may seem like a narrow set of motives, the fracture over Europe was much more than that: it was a symptom of a much deeper set of divisions, the likes of which no existing party of government could paper over.

The second striking aspect of these analyses is that the good, more comprehensive ones all read like chronicles of a death foretold. The Evans and Menon book is a case in point: there may be good story-telling and judicious use of data involved in creating this teleological sense of a "Brexit inevitability", but the overwhelming feeling at the end of the volume, is that the writing had been on the wall for a very long time and that – as a rejoinder to the point above – it is the particular mix of economic pressures, cultural transformations, and the lack of institutional and political outlets for all of these, that conspired to deliver the result of June 2016.

But what else is going on?

The strange combination of shock at the result whilst also giving in to rather teleological interpretations, is interesting. It suggests an awareness that aside from the historical evolution of populist ideas through various political parties, and aside from the role of shifting preferences (as shaped by a rise in inequality, the impact of austerity from 2010, as well as the impact of European migration into the UK – an impact that was manipulated but is no less real) – aside from all of this, there is a suspicion that something far more deeply buried, and far more structural to UK politics has been brought to the surface.

---

3. This was brought home to me several times by senior Conservative politicians, who in fact seemed almost stunned by their own loyalty to the party during trying times.

The empire strikes back

For a number of authors, the role of empire – and loss of empire – is key to understanding the vote to leave the EU. For Danny Dorling and Sally Tomlinson, for instance, "in the near future the EU referendum will become widely recognized and understood as part of the last vestiges of empire working their way out of the British psyche" (Dorling & Tomlinson 2019: 3). Their argument is straightforward: Britain found it extremely hard to come to terms with its loss of empire. To paper over the cracks, it created the Commonwealth. Not only did the "Mother Country" become less and less important in the world, but no amount of rebranding along Commonwealth lines would long dissimulate the fact that, as the various former colonies gained independence, the terms of trade with Britain changed in their favour, not in Britain's. The result was more expensive goods and more expensive labour. As a result, people felt poorer, and were encouraged to blame immigrants. Anthony Barnett makes a related point in his book *The Lure of Greatness*, that as the Commonwealth did not deliver on trade, the UK turned to the European Union: if the empire was over, then the EU would have to do. Barnett's argument is that joining the EU was always perceived as second best, or even as a capitulation (Barnett 2017). And, to make matters worse, a capitulation to a club that was borne of the ashes of the Second World War; borne, in other words, of an alliance of nations to which Britain felt vastly superior because it had helped to save them. Joining the EU, in a word, was always a bit *infra dignitatem*. Second best. At best.

Both of these accounts are persuasive: the first focuses on the role of class and inequality; the second on the role of an ingrained imagined superiority. But to some extent, they do not necessarily answer the question of why, at this particular point, a party such as UKIP was able to manipulate this longstanding wound in the British psyche. What enables this fissure to come to the surface and turn into a tectonic political shift? What mobilized people so successfully when concerns about the EU tended to barely make it into people's lists of their top 10 worries a couple of years before the referendum? There are three answers here: first, money; second, manipulation via social media and the tabloids; and third, and most importantly, the appeal to the authentic nation.

Money, interference and the manipulation of social media

To some extent this is the least interesting aspect of British populism and its key manifestation in the form of Brexit. It is hugely important in terms of getting the "Leave" vote over the line, but it is not that important in terms of the unleashing of populism via UKIP and the Brexit referendum because it is about marginality, which in fact is not the ideological story.

It is worth pointing out, as others have, that the 2016 referendum is largely thought to have been the first "digital" referendum. As Andrew Mullen writes "Both the official Leave ('Vote Leave') and Remain ('Britain Stronger in Europe') campaigns applied key aspects of the successful Obama Model developed during the 2008 and 2012 US Presidential Elections – more specifically big data mining, data analytics, micro-targeting and social media – in an attempt to identify and then mobilize their respective supporters" (Mullen 2016: 89). And it is also worth pointing out that campaign funding got murky, to say the least. Each campaign received a £600,000 government grant, as well as donations from both businesses and private individuals. The Leave campaign, UKIP and a number of other Leave-promoting organizations are, as I write, being investigated for over-spending. More seriously, a criminal investigation has been opened against the (unofficial) Leave campaign (Leave.EU) led by Nigel Farage and ostensibly funded by Arron Banks (a major UKIP donor); the criminal investigation concerns the provenance of the funds. The focus is on £2 million reported to have been lent to Better for the Country (BFTC), a company that was used to finance Leave.EU, and £6 million more, reportedly provided to the organization on behalf of Leave.EU, by Banks.[4] The implication being that the origin of the funds could be a foreign power, thereby making them illegal.[5]

---

4. C. Cadwalladr, "Leave.EU, Arron Banks and new questions about referendum funding", *The Guardian*, 14 April 2018. Available at:https://www.theguardian.com/politics/2018/apr/14/leave-eu-arron-banks-new-question-referendum-funded-brexit-cambridge-analytica (accessed 22 March 2019).

5. C. Cadwalladr, "Arron Banks, Brexit and the Russian Connection", *The Guardian*, 16 June 2018. Available at: https://www.theguardian.com/uk-news/2018/jun/16/arron-banks-nigel-farage-leave-brexit-russia-connection (accesses 22 March 2019).

Finally, the use of big-data mining (drawing upon canvassing returns, social media traffic, voter records and other sources such as consumer databases) as well as the use of the internet and social media for intelligence-gathering purposes and to create personalized voter profiles, gave rise to a level of manipulation (and potential criminality given that data was apparently shared without consent or knowledge) probably never seen before in Europe. It was rapidly apparent that the Leave campaign had been more successful in its micro-targeting. But it only came to light much later, through an investigation by *Observer* journalist Carole Cadwalladr, that £3.9 million was spent by VoteLeave (the official Leave campaign) on Canada-based firm AggregateIQ to harvest data about Britons on Facebook and then target them with personalised adverts.[6] And AggregateIQ appears to be closely linked to Cambridge Analytica, the political campaigning firm funded by American billionaire Robert Mercer (who helped get Donald Trump elected). The point here is that the Leave.EU campaign is now held to have committed offences under the Political Parties, Elections and Referendums Act (PPERA 2000),[7] and more to the point a significant portion of the public feel that a global plutocracy is using technology to sway elections in ways that they were unaware of. The fact that this global plutocracy's arc of action seems to tend toward the Trumps of this world and toward referendums that get in the way of the integrity of international organizations such as the EU is extremely worrisome, but only tangential to my focus.

---

6. C.Cadwalladr,https://www.theguardian.com/technology/2017/may/07/the-great-british-brexit-robbery-hijacked-democracy

7. The Electoral Commission found the unofficial Leave campaign had overspent, failed to declare their sources of funding, and inaccurately reported three separate loans. The Commission also reported reasonable grounds to suspect that the responsible person for Leave.EU committed offences under PPERA and she has therefore been referred to the Metropolitan Police. As for the official Leave Campaign, it also exceeded its spending limits, has refused to cooperate in the investigation, and is thought by the Commission to have committed "serious breaches of the laws put in place by parliament to ensure fairness and transparency at elections and referendums"; see https://www.electoralcommission.org.uk/i-am-a/journalist/electoral-commission-media-centre/party-and-election-finance-to-keep/vote-leave-fined-and-referred-to-the-police-for-breaking-electoral-law (accessed 22 March 2019) and "Report on an investigation in respect of the Leave.EU group Limited", 11 May 2018 at https://www.electoralcommission.org.uk/__data/assets/pdf_file/0018/243009/Report-on-Investigation-Leave.EU.pdf (accessed 22 March 2019).

What is more relevant here is, first, that the polarization created by such methods is undoubtedly a part of the electoral success of populist parties. Such polarization has a number of important consequences: it creates the impression that the other side is not just a political opponent but an enemy to be beaten at all cost, and by all means necessary. It is a zero-sum game (and the bluntness of an instrument such as a referendum reinforces that impression), in part because the other is depicted as an enemy of both common sense, but also of morality. This transformation from opponent to enemy creates the illusion that rules don't apply, that any tactic is warranted. Thereby, de facto, unleashing the potential for violence. Sometimes physical, almost always verbal. It is not a campaign, it is a crusade. The second consequence is that it creates the conditions for trauma: whoever loses is beaten. And is rejected by the majority. This means that the winner must carry that responsibility, and that the loser must carry the shame. In a sense, this signals the complete breakdown of the possibility of political community as we know it. And plays into the hands of populism's Manichean world view.

The role of the tabloids

But the main connection to populism is elsewhere. It is in part in decades of tabloid culture designed in opposition to elites and that reflects, perpetrates and yet pretends to criticize a rigidly maintained class system. Whilst in many other western democracies and certainly in our case studies, populists needed to bring the divide between the people and the elite into existence, British populism (some would argue that this is mainly English populism) found the terrain well-prepared by tabloids. In the tabloids (especially those on the right of the political spectrum – *The Daily Express*, *The Sun* and the *Daily Mail* – but not only), those key populist ideas about corrupt elites and their acts of betrayal against the people, the value of the people's instinct and common sense (generally expressed through outrage or pity – or one and then the other in a matter of hours), the need to protect the nation's integrity against interlopers (no matter how useful they might pretend to be) had been alive and well for over a century in some cases (but certainly since the 1960s in the case of *The Sun*). Above all the tabloids and their culture was one where the authentically British "cheeky-chappie" thrived, spoke his mind, gave in to his baser instincts, much as he would voice his pride in his nation. Tabloids were the authentic home of the authentic people and Europe was one more elite project against which to rebel, because it was thought of as anathema to Britain's people. Tabloid impact has been entirely overshadowed by the role of social media and then social media scandals (indeed it is striking how little has been written about their role in the referendum campaign and since). One rare piece by Levy, Aslan and Bironzoa (2016) does point to some striking statistics: they document that press coverage across the board was heavily biased in favour of Leave and tabloid coverage even more so (75% of *Daily Express*'s coverage was pro-Leave, as was 61% of the *Daily Mail*'s). Once circulation is taken into account the authors conclude that 80 per cent of voters were reading a Leave newspaper (Levy, Aslan & Bironzo 2016: 33).

This tabloid influence and its emphasis on authentic Britishness as instinctive, irreverent and against the elite paved the way for British populism. The emphasis in particular on speaking one's mind and on not being ashamed of instinctive reactions that went against what was seen as an elite norm dovetails rather well with an internet culture that encourages immediate reactions, immediate likes and dislikes and arguments that could fit into 140 characters (280 characters happened later in Autumn 2017). Long before Facebook encouraged us to post everything we did, Instagram to memorialize everything we ate, Twitter to share everything we think, and reality TV to exhibit … everything, the tabloids were prepping Britain's political culture for the great populist onslaught by promoting a vision of society divided between the corrupt fools that ruled the country and the real people who knew what was what and were not ashamed to say it.

But as the culture of the internet collided with that of tabloid Britain, populist politics was handed a golden opportunity that Nigel Farage made the most of. To some extent by focusing on one issue (Europe and leaving it) and one that is at the heart of Conservative Party tensions, Farage picked lower-hanging fruit than his European counterparts whose anti-European terrain is not quite so well ploughed. Farage simply exploited what was already there, and in a context in which austerity made blaming both elites and "the immigrants they let in" much easier: things were falling apart, we were unrecognisable to ourselves. UKIP and its Leave campaign reminded people of who they "really were". For the first time the appeal to authenticity properly crept into UK – and more specifically, English – politics.

Authentic Britain

All of the developments outlined above point to the importance of authenticity in British populist discourse and ideology. This authenticity takes three forms: revelation and accusations, disruption, and lying.

Revelation and accusation

One of the first weapons used by UKIP, and Farage specifically, is broad-brush accusations against elites, and more specifically European elites. There are countless instances in which Farage levels accusations against his fellow MEPs: of being "faux nationalists", of "faux outrage", of "hysteria" (with regard to Trump's immigration rules for example). Farage's accusation, of course, is one of hypocrisy: for Farage such displays by MEPs are manufactured outrage over the fate of democracy by people he considers to be "faux democrats"; and the accusation of hypocrisy allows Farage to adopt a particularly effective counterstance as a result: the mode of "private" conversation – apparently stripped of any artifice – with his followers, his audience, "right-thinking people" with whom he can share a truth. Just him, and you, and several million other followers/audience members. That illusion of a truth, whispered straight into your ear, is designed to make that privileged relationship between the populist politician and his followers seem exclusive, confessional, intimate. The impression of a direct relationship that is mediated by no one or anything is at the heart of the promise, and of the strategy.

One, bona fide, documentary (made by Channel 4 in June 2017), follows Farage around the European Parliament building. Farage makes a great show of getting lost, of being confused by the number of doors, and by the endless hallways. The nature of the building is designed it seems to keep ordinary people like him (even those who practice it regularly) in a state of confusion.[8] It is almost a conspiracy. The EU, and all its personnel and symbols, are accused of inaccessibility and dissimulation – a cardinal sin. The question that Farage leaves hanging is whether this is the result of incompetence or whether it is by design.

---

8. "Nigel Farage: Who Are You", Channel 4 documentary. Available at: https://www. youtube.com/watch?v=1QsDnCxFgV4 (accessed 22 March 2019).

As for Farage, he plays the part of the hapless pawn in this byzantine game. Speaking straight to camera and maintaining a dialogue with his audience, with whom he is sharing a secret and exposing a truth that only they can understand, despite the best efforts of the EU to bamboozle him.

Added to this staging of the other side's opacity, and therefore what is presented as its natural tendency toward corruption and stitch-up, is the spontaneity and disruption that UKIP is willing to stage as proof of its own authenticity. Transgression of normal, or accepted, institutional behaviour is a regular occurrence: the breaking of the norm is the norm. Politically incorrect statements, Tweets designed to raise the political temperature ("Sparks will fly" Farage often predicts, just before making them fly himself); all of these are designed to disrupt and highlight the party's fundamentally different nature: its spontaneity, and the fact that unlike all the other parties it is neither in thrall to the media, nor to the institutions they, UKIP, despise.

Disruption and lying

Much of the arsenal is, as it is for other populist parties, designed to create disbelief ("I cannot believe he said that out loud"), then a frisson of recognition ("well, let's be honest that's what I think too") and then gratitude ("I'm glad someone has had the courage to say it – and in plain English"). Farage's infamous speech in the European Parliament on Herman Van Rompuy's appointment as president of the European Council, in which he opens with: "you are very dangerous people, you should all be fired"; followed by a direct attack on Van Rompuy: "I do not want to be rude, but you have the charisma of a damp rag and the appearance of a low-grade bank clerk".[9] Such speeches are the kind of behaviour that contribute to the impression that (1) Farage is pandering to no one (he is not "adjusting his message") and therefore, the conclusion goes, he is who he says he is and he truly must have the people's interest at heart; and (2) he is speaking in ways that are the true spirit of the nation: cheeky, unbowed, unrestrained. It may be vulgar, but there

---

9. Nigel Farage, "Who is Herman Van Rompuy" speech, European Parliament, 25 February 2010.

is a glimmer of recognition of one's baser self. And that works as a powerful form of reassurance, either because he is doing what most would
never have the nerve to do, or precisely because he is doing exactly
what they would want to do. The leader at that point knows the people's
secrets, and carries them out on their behalf. There are very few relationships in life in which this fantasy is realized. And probably none in
adult life.

There are dozens of examples of such behaviour and they all follow
a similar pattern. But its most riveting aspect is not the performance of
the authentic people, it is the fact that this authenticity relies in great
part on lying. Particularly as the referendum campaign got under way,
the authentic display of nationhood became more and more bound to
telling bigger and bigger lies. I have highlighted earlier the role of lies –
and particularly "common knowledge lies" (those that everyone knows
are lies) – as the great proof that one is willing to upend the norms of
politics entirely. In May 2016 the House of Commons Treasury Select
Committee complained that "The arms race of ever more lurid claims
and counter-claims made by both the leave and remain sides is not just
confusing the public. It is impoverishing political debate. Today is the
first day of the main campaign. It needs to begin with an amnesty on
misleading, and at times bogus, claims. The public are thoroughly fed
up with them. The public are right". And it followed with the Committee
finding Vote Leave's core campaign number – the idea that leaving the
EU would give the country a £350 million a week fiscal windfall to
spend on hospitals and schools – "highly misleading". The figure, and
the suggestion that this money could and should be spent on the NHS,
decorated Vote Leave's "battle bus". The Committee found that Vote
Leave's persistence with this claim to be "deeply troubling".[10]

And shortly after that, former PM John Major made an angry public
intervention declaring that the British public were being misled. Some
authors have even noted that "[what] the EU referendum exposed was
the inability of the British political system to enforce even the most
basic requirements in relation to publicly-funded information campaigns" and go on to suggest that the level of debate was so misleading

---

10. Comments by the Rt. Hon. Andrew Tyrie MP, Chairman of the Treasury Select
Committee, on The Treasury Committee report "The economic and financial costs
and benefits of the UK's EU membership", 27 May 2016.

that there needed to be a new code of conduct (Renwick, Flinders & Jennings 2016: 31).

This is all true, but to some extent, it is missing the point. The lies were not about hiding the truth. The lies were about telling the lies. About showing that being true to yourself matters more than being true to your word. Pushing the boat so far out in rhetorical terms so as to create one overwhelming impression: we will do anything and say anything to make this happen. Who's with us?

And this is the final constitutive move: a big part of the audience goes along with the lie and they become authentic and brave too. And not necessarily because they believe the lies. It is interesting that one MORI poll of 2015 asked voters how much they believed of what politicians were promising on the campaign trail, the result was that only 9 per cent believed any of the promises by any of the parties (cited in Evans & Menon 2017: 82). In the context of the EU referendum and the £350 million NHS windfall, recent research by MORI and King's College Policy Institute, suggests that 42 per cent of the people who had heard of the claim still believe it is true (KCPL 2018). The disparity between these two figures highlights a number of things: the fact that in the context of the EU referendum, voters might have been less cynical or, as other research has highlighted, most people came to the referendum campaign with an already formed view which made them perhaps less prone to argue with "their own side". But perhaps above all, it suggests that what was at play in the referendum campaign was a question of identity as framed by populist politics, one in which believing in the lie was not about accepting or rejecting information, but signing up to be a part of a club with a specific identity (not so bothered by facts and expertise, and much more interested in breaking free of traditional political norms).

Taking back control

The final paradox is that, what appears to be a complete lack of control – making things up, insulting one's partners and allies, and misleading one's own voters – is actually part of a grand promise to "Take Back Control". This slogan which has become emblematic of this moment of British politics, sums up many of the fantasies that underpin populism across Europe. It suggests first and foremost a capacity to act – in the face of decades of TINA. It is, in its most benign form, a renewed desire for personal political efficacy. But is also, in this context, wresting back sovereignty: over borders, money, decisions. Even if all of these might be weakened, the promise is one of control through isolation. For many who watched in horror, the promise of "taking back control" was a threat of self-harm. But for others, taking back control was (and is) the phrase of a victim, or a hostage shaking off Stockholm syndrome. An act of immediate and palpable consequences and of authenticity (we know who we are, the real people of Britain). On an island defined over the past few decades by its increasingly mixed population and multicultural practices, by its cosmopolitan financial centre versus its provincial towns, taking back control was the ultimate fantasy of omnipotence. And when everything except politics promises you a say, a view, an impact, a choice, a voice – the lure of the referendum was too much to resist.

Nigel Farage benefited at least as much from the decades-old work of the tabloid as he did from social media (though he does have 1.2 million followers on Twitter). But the tabloids in the past few years, have benefited from the work of social media: the UK has one of the world's highest levels of internet penetration (95% in June 2018), and by far one of the largest Facebook user communities in the world, with 44 million Facebook users in June 2017 (the next largest is France, far behind on 33 million, and then Italy on 30 million). What matters here is that both types of media – tabloid and social – shape citizen expectations, and more to the point skew them towards ideas and means that are at the heart of populism.

7

Populism and the new political subject

A case of the missing person

What these four cases illustrate is that certain key ideas matter: populism is not just "a version of …" and crucially, that these ideas matter in their relationship to one another. Taken together they are greater than the sum of their parts, and it is that relational logic between them that imparts its dynamics to populist politics. And citizens seem to have become far more responsive to them. Some of the approaches we initially looked at take into account that values ebb and flow, and of course events and developments shape them. But no approach seems to do justice to the new link between citizen demands for directness, immediacy and transparency, what we have called authenticity.

In fact, in most approaches there is only a vague sense of the citizen, or political subject. Analysts have been a little thin on the relational side of populism, and extremely thin on what some might call the "demand side" of populism. Yet, there may be crisis, and there may be discourses, and there may be ideas, but someone has to be in the mood to respond to them.

A populist profile?

Most studies that try to look at populist "voters" focus on demographics, hoping that through a deductive enterprise a better sense of a "populist voter" might emerge. In a Counterpoint pamphlet, for instance, my colleagues and I looked at the characteristics of populist party voters in Europe and tried to draw out correlations between education, or income or employment status, gender, etc, and a propensity to vote for a populist party (Fieschi, Morris & Caballero-Sosa 2012). But the best one can do with such numbers – and this is by no means useless – is to draw correlations between support for a populist party and voters with these characteristics. This can be helpful in terms of thinking about voting behaviour, but in fact it tells us little about the motivations of these voters. This is also because voters seem increasingly diverse: what used to be a mainly male voting base, for example, has dramatically evolved; and voters' levels of income and life characteristics are more varied than they used to be, as populism has become more successful and captured more voters.

Other perspectives have also emerged based essentially on psychological portraits. Many of these studies focus on what kind of "psychological profile" can account for support for populist politics. There are a number of studies that attempt to correlate votes for populist parties or leaders with authoritarian personality traits for instance (MacWilliams 2016), or with other personality traits such as narcissism (Marchlewska *et al.* 2018), or with in-group/out-group behaviour (Oliver & Rahn 2016).

But, while one set of studies explores the populist offer comprehensively, and the other, smaller set, explores what appears to be a "hardwired" human subject pre-disposed to the populist offer, there is very little that looks at how human beings as political subjects and in their political expectations might have evolved to make them so susceptible to the populist offer. The argument here is that while it is important to understand the offer itself (its components, its instruments, its vehicles, and the events that render it more powerful and convincing), understanding what made these ideas stick at a particular point and time – when in fact, many have been around for much longer – is also quite important.

A more relational approach: populism as political style

A more interesting way into an understanding of populism is to think of it as what Benjamin Moffitt and Simon Tormey (2014) call a "political style" (see also Moffitt 2016). In their work (and even more directly so in Moffitt's work) populism is not an ideology (it is not "a thing"), nor is it a way of organizing politics, but rather it is about how the relationship between people and politics is performed. This approach at least looks not just at a passive citizen, or a never-ending supply of populist offers, but rather at how the two interact:

> In our case, when it comes to the populist political style, we are interested in how the performances of those involved influence the relationship between the populist leader and 'the people', and vice versa. Such an understanding eschews the traditional distinction between style and content that other approaches inherently rely on: we are not purely interested in the 'content' of so-called populist ideology, or just the organizational forms of political logic that populism might utilize, but rather how the performative repertoires of populist leaders and their followers interact, and how this affects their relationship. (Moffitt & Tormey 2014: 387–8)

This approach is useful: it reminds us that this is about politics, and so it is about relationships of power. In the case of populism, the fact that leaders play such a prominent role in people's political imagination is something that needs to be taken into account. Finding a way of doing so that doesn't reduce populism to charismatic leadership, but rather frames it as a performed relationship between a leader and their followers is useful for a better understanding of political leadership. And to some extent, therein lies its problem: it works better as an explanation of contemporary political leadership in what are "spectacular times" – in the original sense – than it does as an explanation of populism. It is true that the performance element of populism creates populism's "people", but to some extent any politics is now performed, and therefore all political styles create their own people, or at least their own community. Populism "performs" in a particular way, and citizens seem more than ever receptive to it. Why?

The bothersome blind-spot remains: we still do not know much about who this political subject is. In all of the approaches above, the citizen has not varied much. Psychological approaches tend to give us a static human being with a set political profile. Most theories that privilege ideas, whilst foundational, tend to posit a political subject that relates to key ideas in a relatively fixed way. That's not to say that they do not change their minds over the course of a lifetime, or evolve in their preferences, but they tend to be depicted as doing so based on the same understanding of these ideas. Michael Freeden's analogy is telling: he compares ideologies to professors' rooms in Oxford colleges. In these rooms, you will always find versions of the same furniture (desk, rug, shelves, paintings, lamps, etc), but each professor arranges it differently. Some of them display art more prominently than others. Some will be prouder of their rugs, whilst in others the only visible thing may be a comfortable chair or their desk. Ideologies are the same, Freeden argues, you can more or less find the same ingredients, the same concepts and ideas in all of them, but their prominence varies. Liberty is centre stage in liberalism, whereas equality might be shoved behind a book-shelf. Equality may dominate in the socialism room, whereas individualism might be in a dark corner.

The point, however, is that Freeden assumes that it is always the same political subject entering the room. The visitor does not fundamentally change, and neither do her expectations. What about the visitor who is looking for something very different? For whom what matters is the view out of the window, or who is in the room next door? Or who wants a tutorial under the apple tree? To some extent all of the approaches we've covered posit a relatively known and stable political subject. Even in the work on performance, which is fundamentally relational, the relationship varies according place and time, but there is no sense in which the voter or the citizen is fundamentally changed, or receptive to fundamentally different ideas.

Yet the case studies tell us that voters are far more susceptible to certain ideas than they ever were: honesty, trust, participation have taken on new meaning through the prism of authenticity. And populists have been best-placed to take advantage of this shift, because authenticity was always a part of the ideological arsenal.

Populism, digital and the self

My aim is not to underplay the role of major events, such as 9/11, or the financial crisis. These have affected people's lives and their political views, in particular their confidence in the capacity of traditional parties to address their worries. There is an obvious correlation between the collapse of social democratic parties in western Europe (and its acceleration over the past decade) for example, and the rise of populist parties on the back of the popular, working-class vote (a working class that has changed dramatically in its make-up and expectations). Nor is it to diminish the relevance of issues such as migration, inequality, etc. Although these, as we indicated earlier on, need to be taken as rather "circumstantial" appeals that tap into something far deeper. But the question remains: what appeal does populism hold to assuage the unease provoked by such events? Why has the financial crisis not triggered much enthusiasm for the traditional radical left? (Corbyn, who *can* be counted as the most traditional of radical left-wingers, is the only such figure, and even then, inside a fragmented and fraying Labour Party). Why is it that when climate change is clearly one of the – if not the – most existentially threatening issue of our time, Green parties seem to have so far, so spectacularly failed to make effective political inroads? The claim that traditional mainstream parties may no longer be fit for purpose is clear, but why has the populist alternative been so much more successful than the rest?

So much more than social media

The transformation that needs to be factored in – and which is the elephant in the room – is the digital transformation and how it fits with populist ideas. This is not an argument about social media use by parties, the depleted attention span of voters, or fake news. Those are all true, but they affect all parties equally. The question here is how – and how come – populist parties and populist politicians have made the most of this (when others clearly have not).

Jamie Bartlett is right when he writes that "populist politics is clickable and shareable content", that "Blogs, Facebook and Twitter are the perfect platform" for someone like Beppe Grillo, because they are an antidote to the dull greyness of mainstream politicians. "With its word-count limits and network sharing there's no time for the boring business of negotiation and compromise online. Digital technology is dichotomous and interactive: a series of discrete packets: 0/1, 'like/do not Like', My Guy/Not My Guy, Evil/Good. It incentivises simplicity and rewards pithiness" (Bartlett 2017: 170–1; see also Rushkoff 2016).

But I want to suggest that there is even more going on than that. That this is not simply that social media encourages a form of behaviour that dovetails with the simplistic message of populism – although it does – nor, even, that populism changes what we want from politicians (less predictable, quicker and more entertaining) – although it does that too; rather I think we are dealing with two things. First, our emotional and psychological connection to each other and to any community, including political community, is changed by the behaviour that digital media activates and encourages. We begin to perceive ourselves differently and to value different things. And second, populism is made up of those core ideas that I've already outlined, that work hand in hand with social media. It is not just a coincidence that populism arises just as we seem more drawn in by shock-statements, more susceptible to fake news and lies, and grow impatient with compromise: it is that populism includes, in its own core ideational make-up, a suspicion of complexity, a disdain for compromise, and a version of authenticity predicated on immediacy and transparency. Populism pre-dates digital, but digital grants it new power, because it transforms us. And it transforms us beyond digital. Our off-line behaviour and outlooks are shaped by it. So, for instance, the UK is a case study in how digital seamlessly integrated with a political culture shaped by tabloids, and tabloids seamlessly reflected the greater appetites for authenticity unleashed by digital. A form of authenticity has always mattered, but digital accelerates this through speed and immediacy.

So, the focus here is on the more profound changes that the digital transformation has unleashed on human expectations, and how these have been reshaped in ways that create a perfect fit for populism's key ideas, and a perfect opportunity for populist politicians. There is no conspiracy here, simply that technological developments have, as they have in the past, opened a grand boulevard for political change, and some political actors were in a better position to take advantage of them. Directness, authenticity, accessibility, a suspicion of complexity, all of these were already there, waiting to be fuelled exponentially by the digital experience that places all of these at the heart of our everyday experience.

Factoring in the unknown knowns

The digital transformation and its impact also need to be factored in through the lens of political analysis, but also through a different one that uses both psychological as well as psychoanalytic concepts.

Making sense of populist politics is not just about making sense of a new political subject reshaped by the circumstances of digital transformation, it is also about what these circumstances are making us remember about ourselves. About, in short, what makes us tick. Things that we have almost forgotten that we know. As Slavoj Žižek points out, picking up on Rumsfeld's famous pronouncement regarding weapons of mass destruction in Iraq, "there are also unknown knowns, that is, there are things we do not know that we know – which is precisely the Freudian unconscious, the 'knowledge which doesn't know itself,' as Lacan used to say" (Žižek 2004). Populism reminds us of what we long for, or secretly hope, or desperately need and will smash anything to get because populism lets all of this erupt onto the political scene: the need to feel recognized, the need to feel understood, the need to feel omnipotent. It also reminds us of the political and social consequences of feeling none of these things despite being promised them. These deep wants escape frameworks of conscious calculation (although not necessarily of reason) but they animate and underpin our political choices and those who offer them to us. Political science has never been very good at incorporating that last part. The unconscious is relegated to the background, and yet it crops up in every policy, in every promise, in every speech, in every one of our reactions. Without being heavy-handed about this here, taking these key human dynamics into account is important because it sheds some light on why we seem so puzzled by populism: part of the fascination with populist politics is that they never cease to surprise us. Populism, because it depends in part on its capacity to disrupt the status quo and up-end norms, never ceases to bring unpredictability back to politics, and more importantly into political analysis. As a social science, political science does not deal especially well with that: its aims are to eradicate that kind of unpredictability. Allowing the unconscious back in, may mean a better understanding of, at least, where that unpredictability might come from. And where it is, actually, quite foreseeable.

When Salvini posts ten updates a day speaking directly into his camera, directly to you; when Wilders shares a joke directly with you because only you "get it"; when Nigel Farage says "this is common sense", "It's not that difficult – we can just leave", it works with followers, not because of some magical charismatic relationship, but because the statement taps into fantasies that are long held but intensely heightened by digital.

Taking both sets of dynamics (how the transformation fits with populist ideas and how it has reshaped us as political subjects) into account is an important complement to the various explanations about why populist ideas have made such deep inroads into our politics. So deep that they will have fundamentally affected the political landscape and, possibly, have ushered in a new template for all ideologies to come.

Brave new digital world

Most studies of politics tend to start with a citizen that is predetermined in her range of political emotions and therefore in her range of preferences and of political repertoires. The result is an understanding of citizens as historically predictable: an influx of migrants makes them more receptive to xenophobic appeals; a downturn in the economy lowers their confidence in their leaders. And when the opposite operates, the reactions are reversed. I am not arguing that migration, belonging, economic hardship or security do not play a role – they certainly do; they are in one sense a political stimulus. But these events are mediated through new channels that, in turn, fundamentally change their impact. So, what feels unfair, or what feels unbearable may have changed. What is acceptable, or unacceptable fluctuates; and so, have the springs of engagement and revolt. The older springs have not necessarily been replaced, but they have been supplemented with new forms of outrage. Just as forms we thought had disappeared for good, are being revived. And digital culture has helped bring all of them to the surface.

There are a great many changes that have affected citizens since the emergence of mass democracy in the twentieth century. And there is a plentiful literature that covers the kind of "disenchantment" with politics that this creates: the decline in confidence in most institutions, the diminished faith placed in political parties and membership thereof, the dented public trust in politicians as well as the accompanying willingness to challenge political authority (see Dalton & Kuechler 1990; Inglehart 1990; Klingemann 1999; Klingemann & Fuchs 1995; Dalton 2007). However incomplete, and however poorly distributed, the twentieth century's great push for egalitarianism transformed politics – and our relationship to it. It did so through political and industrial technology set in motion by the revolutionary intellectual, political, social and economic movements of the Enlightenment. All of which were rooted in a conception of the state, and of communities of citizens fashioned by what British-American political historian Benedict Anderson called "print capitalism". There is a danger of infinite regress in making such historical parallels, but they are a valuable perspective from which to evaluate our own era of technological revolution and its political impact. A parallel that goes far beyond narrow partisan issues and social media use.

In 1983 Anderson wrote what is perhaps still the most cogent and detailed explanation of the transformations ushered in by "print cap-italism" (Anderson 1991). Print capitalism, he argued, is what made "imagined communities" possible. In other words, it enabled human beings to think of themselves as connected despite time and distance outside the concept of spiritual communities, for the first time.

The transformations of the digital revolution also create new visions of the self. It is the very nature of human experience that is being refash-ioned, so we should not be surprised that this tests the limits (and quite possibly leads to the annihilation) of our current institutional order, much as print capitalism annihilated the institutions of feudalism.

Our understanding of populism – its ideological power, its capac-ity to affect the future – depends on a greater awareness of the deep psychological transformations that we are undergoing and how these are reshaping our general attitudes and expectations vis-à-vis politics and our political leaders. It also depends on a greater awareness of the new or reinvigorated political fantasies these transformations lead us to harbour; expectations and fantasies that can easily be preyed upon by any party, but in particular by those for whom speaking what usu-ally remains "unspoken" has particular political purchase. What does it mean when an entire campaign is run on the slogan "Take back con-trol!"? Or when a party's electoral slogan is "Vote for yourself"? What does that tap into?

The best place to start therefore, is with what new dynamics the dig-ital revolution seems to have imparted on our lives and their knock-on effects on citizens' political views, their expectations and, ultimately, their behaviour.

What is digital, what does it do and why it matter? A quick recap

For all our everyday pronouncements about the impact of digital tech-nology, the source of this impact often remains unspecified. For the sake of clarity, let's specify why digital differs so fundamentally from analogue.

The main characteristic of digital technology is that it works with data (binary code) rather than physical signals (whether that is sound waves, electrical impulses, or the hands of a watch). This means that unlike analogue technology, digital technology creates a universal language that can be used by anyone, anywhere. The important point here is that the universality of the code is what makes for the ubiquity of use, the resulting speed of connection and the ease of interconnection across media. And that has changed everything. In a nutshell: the impression is one of simplicity and immediacy.

This technological change could not but reshape our emotional landscapes: we now live our lives differently. We are social beings (or at least, we have been), and if digital provides us with seemingly endless opportunities to connect to more people, goods, places, ideas, news, faster than ever, and in new ways, then it is right to think about how such changes would affect the way that we might relate to our leaders and institutions, but even more broadly how we understand ourselves as part of a society or a political community.

The point, therefore, is to look beyond the countless analyses of whether or not social media is a "good" or a "bad" thing, beyond whether or not populist parties are "good at using Facebook", and take a deeper look at how digital has made us so much more receptive to populism's core promises by changing our expectations. In particular our expectations concerning immediacy, simplicity and transparency.

The experience of ease and speed

The everyday manifestations of digital communication (the speed with which it delivers information and apparent ease with which we transmit and receive it – directly and with little effort – and as if distances no longer existed) is actually deceptive, and that trick is at the heart of the political transformation we are in, because by heightening our expectations of ease and speed it reshapes how we interact with the world, including, of course, the political world.

By creating the illusion of connecting everything immediately and giving us the power to connect to others who we do not know (and vice-versa), social media creates a model in which our relationships feel instant (we reach out to strangers, they answer back, networks appear and disappear, communities emerge and wane with a few clicks of a mouse) and our own personal relevance can seem both infinite and central.

More importantly, the fact that all this feels simple and immediate tends to erase the complexity that underpins human interactions: it smooths over uncertainty, dissimulates complexity, and tries to minimize misunderstandings. Yet the ease of this predictable and "complexity-free" experience is superficial: it exists only in terms of how the layperson perceives it, but everything about it is carefully and purposely constructed by the tech industry and with great effort. "Clunkiness" is a death-sentence and to be avoided at all costs. Tech companies, and their products, create the impression that connecting is simple, universal to the point of being direct and, therefore paradoxically, unmediated by either distance or effort. But we know that this is not only a highly misleading experience, but also that it creates potentially more misunderstanding and uncertainty. But what I am particularly interested in is the three expectations that it creates in terms of our relationships to others, whether they be personal, social, or political.

New expectations: effortless, direct, immediate

We have come to expect effortlessness, directness and immediacy, in the sense that we demand simple interactions, truthful and spontaneous exchanges, and immediate connection and reactions.

First, there is a higher value placed on simplicity because the seamlessness and ease of interactions and transactions contribute to the suspicion that anything that cannot be known or understood easily and instantly is, at best, not being explained well, or worse, being purposefully dissimulated or manipulated to seem more complicated than it is.[1] There is but an easy step between this glorification of simplicity to

---

1. A good example of the sacralization of simplicity is the explosion of TED Talks as a medium. Not only do they suggest that knowledge comes in little information packets, much like code; they also contribute to the widespread sense that access to knowledge resides almost exclusively in the fluency and rehearsed spontaneity of the "talker". My point is not meant to take away from the pleasure of well

a disdain for, and suspicion of, complexity. If so much can be so simple, then the exceptions to that rule are either suspect or the result of incompetence.

Secondly, there is a heightened expectation of directness which leads to an expectation of truthfulness. We imagine that we can see things as they are, and – equally important – that we can be seen as we truly are.[2] Bizarrely, the unfiltered but relentlessly curated profile – mine or someone else's – feels more accurate and genuine than what might be understood in real-life (RL) exchanges that are messier and more prone to misunderstanding. In her volume *Alone Together*, Sherry Turkle tracks young people who look forward to "finally broadcasting their real selves" on Facebook (as though this was their true birth), when they have agonized over replies to Snapchat messages for several hours in an attempt to make them sound "really spontaneous".

Thirdly, there is an expectation of immediacy of connection and response. The speed of access, speed of connection, speed of responses creates a level of permanent impatience, as well as, conversely, a febrility when the anticipated response or reaction is slower than anticipated. Of course, reality is far more paradoxical. Perhaps in part because of the widespread currency of these expectations, lived reality is experienced as consistently falling short of them. Hence the growing frustration upon which populist politics capitalize.

---

explained, witty, gripping talks that familiarize us with areas we knew little or nothing about; but, the message is, in part, that there is little that we cannot know through 10-minute, bite-sized chunks. And, more to the point, little that cannot be explained to match. The fact that the talkers are recognized experts in their field, and that the talks are hyper-rehearsed and scripted, is systematically hidden through Ted's careful curation of informality and spontaneity. The impression is that this is effortless. Again, making such expertise accessible is laudable and useful, but the dissimulation of the hard work of acquiring expertise, is what contributes to its downgrading. And perhaps more to the point, contributes to the general illusion that understanding can be effortless, and that spontaneity is the only value; a spontaneity that, ironically, needs to be pursued quite relentlessly.

2. Paradoxically, the anonymity can feel as though it is most conducive to honesty and spontaneity. Aaron Ben-Ze'ev (2004) was an early documenter of the manner in which anonymity can create an overwhelming sense of intimacy.

The digital citizen and the fantasy of radical transparency

Finally, these heightened expectations give rise to a fantasy[3] – a form of wakeful wishful thinking that fulfils a deep set of desires, but has little bearing on reality – that we might call of "radical transparency": this fantasy encompasses both our wish to be understood without having to struggle to explain ourselves and to be understood as authentically as possible, without artifice; but also its mirror impulse: the desire to make sense of things (information, situations, reactions) and people (our fellow citizens, our leaders, celebrities and ordinary others) effortlessly.

Overall, this fantasy of radical transparency is one of a frustration-free existence. In which responses (including policy responses) are swift, effective, easily understandable and deployable; based on both common sense and instinct, both of which bypass the need for explanation. Seen through the lens of this fantasy of radical transparency, the demand is for politics to privilege the following key attributes on which populism easily builds.

Readable citizens

One of the cornerstones of this political fantasy is the desire to be truly understood and accepted, to be "got" – warts and all – with little explaining on our part. This applies first and foremost to our fellow citizens, who should be naturally "in sync" with us. This is how Adam Phillips sums it up: "Groups of people tend to define themselves, by the things they all get. Outsiders do not get it, and if or when they do, it is a shock to the system (as all immigrants know). Such moments of recognition, when connections are suddenly sprung – when something is said that is something in common – always promise an abundance; They seem to push on an open door" (Phillips 2012: 46). A politics that privileges this all the time, as populism promises to do, taps into something extremely powerful.

The "dream of like-mindedness", as Phillips puts it, is a dream about a group of people, or a couple, in which the possibility of not getting it

---

3. Perhaps even what psychoanalysts call a "phantasy", because we do not necessarily know that we are in the grip of it.

– indeed the whole issue of not getting it – has disappeared (*ibid.*: 54). In other words, where one of our worst fears – of being left out, of not being in on the joke – has been assuaged, abolished. The idea of authenticity at the heart of populism is also a promise to be "got". It is more than about a shared culture, or even about a shared character (which would broadly fall under "nationalism"), it is of the order of "assumption". Digital culture heightens that assumption, heightens its importance in our lives and promises to make it reality in every aspect of our lives. In part by gradually isolating us from those who think differently and therefore might raise the possibility of not "being got", or "getting it".

This kind of wordless understanding places a premium on natural communities, and relatively homogenous ones at that. Communities whose politics and policies will not be held up or held hostage by the negotiation and bargaining that diversity inevitably demands; communities in which a mere aggregation of preferences suffices, instead of the elaborate translation and interpretation that a multitude of languages, viewpoints and backgrounds inevitably generates in democracies. The role of this wordless understanding of each other cannot be overstated. In the conversations, interviews, focus groups, formal and informal, that I have held over the years, this is one of the gripes that comes up again and again – across Europe. "Why do I have to explain the obvious? After all, this is my home, 'they' just have to figure it out". And all populist politics pander to that: we know who we are, and we don't have to think about it.

Finally, this demand for an instantly readable and familiar – because completely transparent – other, (whose profiles are accessible, whose likes and dislikes are on display, whose preferences, habits and pet-peeves are all out there to be known), plays directly into the hands of a politics of instinct. Such politics has little or no truck with the effort associated with making one's self intelligible, or with elaborating explanations for policy. It creates voters and supporters who are encouraged to trust their instinct and common sense and bypass ambivalence, nuance or anything that might be the product of hesitation. One's measure is taken not by what one says, but what immediate conviction one can display. That conviction is taken as the proof that you belong, because you are authentic.

A leader flawed like us

The populist leadership element needs to be understood in the context of a relationship based on the fantasy of radical transparency, that the leader's role in a populist party or movement is not necessarily about strength, or even about that elusive charisma, a kind of magnetism that compels people to listen and to follow. Rather, in the relationship between the people and the populist leader what truly matters is the recognition, and celebration, of one's flawed self: it is the leader's willingness to project the people into existence as they see themselves, and the people's willingness to recognize themselves in the leader's qualities, but also in their flaws. It is this last part that I think eludes much populism analysis. Populist leadership is about the rejection of mainstream politics' most sacred cows, chief amongst them virtue, and more specifically honesty. This is where the paradoxical quality of populist leadership comes in: it is based not on honesty and sincerity (to do as you say you will) but on authenticity to be as you say you are. One of us, just like us, including in our imperfections.

The fantasy of radical transparency is what makes authenticity – fuelled by digital – such an important component of populism. And it helps explain why lying fulfils a very important and specific role; in fact what analysts and observers often hold as populism's Achilles' heel – that the lies will eventually cause the downfall – is the weapon of choice. As pointed out by Hahl, Kim & Sivan (2018) even though people claim to value trustworthiness, in politics this is difficult. People also assume that politicians will "say anything to get elected", in other words that they are willing to pander in order to get votes. Populist politicians will typically choose to come across as mavericks: they will not only tell lies that the authors characterize as "special access lies" (the person is lying, but no one could know that they are), but they will very routinely tell "common knowledge lies" (everyone knows that this is not true) (*ibid.*: 4–6). The common knowledge lies mark out the populist as a real maverick; as someone who is willing to take chances in order to get elected. And perhaps, is speaking a repressed truth. By flagrantly violating the rules of the establishment they show that they really are on the side of the disenfranchised community. In this respect the populist politician can be regarded as authentic even if they are insincere and dishonest. And being caught in a lie can even provide a golden opportunity to come across as "truly and reliably human", as opposed to the bloodless bureaucrats of mainstream politics.

Transparent decision-making

Conversely, if the conceit of this fantasy is that one can be understood without having to explain, and if leaders can be known directly and in all their flawed humanity, then the same logic applies to decisions and policy. Decisions should make sense and be understood effortlessly. The assumption is that all information can be made available, and there is no reason why the public should not be in the immediate position to make sense of it immediately. Any reference to complexity, or mere complication due to technical aspects, for instance, is rejected. The hallmark of truth, in this scheme, is that it is easily accessible. It should not require any explanation or translation by experts: because that could imply tampering or manipulation.

This is where the notion of common sense becomes crucial. Common sense in this context is the basic capacity to make sense of information, or a situation, without having to resort to forms of expertise or even much knowledge. Displaying common sense, as opposed to expertise or intellect, means activating a trait that is a combination of community wisdom (made up of values and that guide the decision-making process) and individual, instinctive discernment – a form of intuition rooted in familiarity and experience. Common sense is therefore always culturally defined and putting it on display, as well as being able to discern it in others, is a fail-proof test that one belongs to a particular community. Common sense is another great proof of one's authentic belonging.

The perils of satisfaction at all costs (or why we need the bumps in the road)

Taken together, what all this points to is not only the elimination of complexity, but the elimination of frustration in every aspect of life, and especially in politics. Immediacy and seamlessness lead us to demand the eradication of waiting, of having to explain, of struggling to make sense. We have not only shifted our expectations, but we no longer cope very well when expectations are not met.

What psychoanalysts refer to as "failure of gratification" – and the rest of us know as frustration – is one of the building blocks of adulthood. In political terms, while it certainly is not my intention to sing a hymn to frustration, it is important to think about what we lose if we no longer expect it or experience bouts of it. Two things spring to mind in the context of politics. The first is that unless some frustration is experienced, we diminish our own capacity to be realistic about what satisfaction feels or looks like. The second and more important problem with the elimination of frustration entirely, is that frustration is, basically, what forces us to think. Without frustration we do not pause, we do not reflect, or adjust. In fact, you could argue that it is mostly under the impetus of frustration that we engage in the kind of critical thinking that allows us to develop a strategy to improve matters, to engage in struggle. Without the capacity to experience and recognize frustration there would be no constructive, progressive politics. We need to feel frustration to know what we want and to pursue it, but both the digital experience and populist politics promise to eliminate it.

This is a perfect storm: digital pretends to eliminate every speed-bump, and populism promises a politics in which authenticity eliminates every possible frustration. The combination of the two conspires to create almost inestimable disappointment and, as a result, a vicious cycle of grievances and frustration. Grievances that are very real: frustrations that have been added to by false promises. The cycle is also often met by more populist promises.

Breaking that cycle – in other words allowing for another political alternative to emerge – is about recognizing what role frustration can play in identifying the real satisfaction of our real needs, rather than sweeping them further under the carpet through more populist promises. But our digital culture has so far done nothing to help that, in fact quite the opposite it has continued to promise even less frustration, even more speed. Yet we know that, as Adam Phillips puts it, paraphrasing Freud, "greed is despair about pleasure" (Phillips 2012: xix).

The paradoxes of the connected self: Connection, compulsion, community and control

The nature of the digital promise means that it gives rise to a host of paradoxes that feed directly into populist politics and few people have explored these paradoxes as thoroughly as Sherry Turkle. In her first book *The Second Self* (1984), which explored how computers were changing our lives, Turkle had begun to track the allure of what she called at the time the "screen self". By the time she began to write *Alone Together* (2011), it had become apparent that there was only one self – rather than two – but that it was undergoing radical alterations.

Her most important insights are those gleaned from the countless conversations she has had with the subjects of her study. Through these she monitors human beings who are increasingly, as she puts it, "alone together"; constantly connected, inevitably a part of something larger than themselves. They are striving for recognition and connection but feel increasingly irrelevant. Turkle starts with herself:

> I like to look at the list of "favorites" on my iPhone contact list and see everyone I cherish. Each is just a tap away. If someone doesn't have time to talk to me, I can text a greeting, and they will know I am thinking of them, caring about them. Looking over recent text exchanges with my friends and family reliably puts me in a good mood. Yet, even such simple pleasures bring compulsions that take me by surprise (Turkle 2011:142).

All of us are in this conundrum: reassured by the connection but often puzzled by the behaviour it triggers in us. The fact is that the more connected we feel, the more compelled we are to check on that connection, often compulsively so. Just as the more reassured we feel by our many contacts, the more vulnerable we feel to abandonment. And whilst we are aware of how central to our lives our families and friends are, we are nevertheless ever more prone to disregarding them while we attempt to tend to everything at once through our connected devices, just as we worry that they will do the same. These impulses and their associated fears are not new, but they are enabled with unprecedented intensity – because on an unprecedented scale – through constant access to communication technology. Just as the technology is uninterrupted, so is the roller-coaster of our elation and anxiety.

These new emotions and the demands and frustrations they create flow into all areas of our lives, including politics. Populism – an ideology built in part on the idea of betrayal – cannot but thrive on this exacerbated promise of recognition and its failure (both political shortcomings – given the mass nature of our institutions – but also its obvious policy failures: austerity politics being an absolute denial of a very basic recognition of one's needs).

One of the final paradoxes to emerge from Turkle's interviews is the simultaneous need to feel that we are at the heart of a network, always surrounded and reassured, always communicating – but increasingly driven by the need to eliminate the risks that necessarily come from such sustained communications. Hence the hours spent curating profiles, polishing replies, editing selfies, and generally striving for impeccable spontaneity and complete authenticity. As Turkle sums it up, "Today, our machine dream is to be never alone but always in control" (*ibid.*: 145).

The aim of achieving control in this maelstrom is both understandable – given how overwhelming these myriad connections can become – and utterly fantastical given the lack of control implied by our heavy reliance on algorithms for much of the dynamic imparted on these networks. The frenzied pursuit of control is a reasonable albeit self-defeating endeavour. And it plays a central part in the political fantasies we entertain.

Next step: populism

As the chasm between fantasy politics and reality politics grows, populism threatens to engulf all available space. The digital promise has conspired to create a political subject who will treat the political realm as an extension of her digital experience: like and dislike, vote and abstain, but also reward and punish driven by expectations that have been dramatically refashioned. And that, so far, political parties have failed to satisfy. The paradox of all this, and the one that populism mercilessly exploits, is that in this fantasy based on directness and the elimination of frustration, our experience of powerlessness, our lack of control over our lives means that we experience record levels of frustration just as we are promised record levels of control. Populism fills that void expertly and relentlessly.

Conclusion: jiu-jitsu politics

This book began with a question regarding how puzzled we are by populist politics: we broadly understand its causes, but we still struggle to understand how and why it works so well, and above all, the particular shape it takes. The answer, I argue, is that populist parties have turned one of the most powerful promises of the Enlightenment – and of democracy – against itself. By making the promise of authenticity core to its appeal, it has been able to harness the promises of democracy and subvert them. It is a kind of political jiu-jitsu, in which rather than using its own force against its democratic opponents, populism has turned the opponent's own force on itself. This hasn't happened by accident: the nature of political expectations has changed fundamentally under the pressures and the promises of the digital revolution. For those of us living in largely democratic states, authenticity has always been an idea central to our politics, but the transformations ushered in by the digital age have made us more receptive to wild promises of authenticity, of transparency and of accessibility. And so, what was one of representative democracy's defining ideas has been exploited to usher in the very antithesis of representative democracy.

It is the fact that populism is so closely related to democracy, that it borrows and subverts its most cherished concepts, applies its recipes, and stretches its logic to extremes that makes it such a powerful ideological opponent. Every time you think you have it pinned it down, it struggles free by stunning you with your own references, your own moves.

The dark matter of authenticity

For a number of people, the idea that authenticity should resurface in such a guise is a particularly bitter pill to swallow. And yet populism's subversive appeal to authenticity seems to have captured the deep tectonic shift that defines this political moment. Authenticity has become both the yardstick by which opposition is judged – a moral yardstick that turns political opponents into amoral, or worse immoral, creatures – but also the defining quality to embody. As G. S. Enli puts it, "it has become a strategy in its own right" (Enli 2016: 133). And as suggested by digital media and psychology experts, it has become an end in itself for the citizen. Being perceived as authentic is, authentically, an aim to be pursued.

Initially – a long time ago – we seemed to be satisfied with striving for sincerity. In his brilliant volume *Sincerity and Authenticity* (1971) Lionel Trilling examines the forces that led sincerity to emerge as a key value in the early modern period as well as those that led to its fall from grace and its replacement with authenticity. The author notes that for much of our histories sincerity "was enough". But sincerity ran out of steam as it became perceived as being true to one's self "only to avoid falsehood to others" (Trilling 1971: 9). The spectacle of sincerity as hypocrisy tipped the scales in favour of a different rapport to the self in which the construction of a self whose internal nature was consistent with its external form and in which the pursuit of that coincidence between the inner self and its public behaviour became of paramount importance: "Authenticity, […] is a private virtue, or still more emphatically, an anti-public one, since it regards all intercourse with other people as potentially deceptive. If sincerity is saying what you mean, authenticity is being what you are" (Kirsch 2008).

As Maiken Umbach and Mathew Humphrey (2017) point out, authenticity is rarely studied as a political concept. Yet, in part through the power of the digital revolution, authenticity has become the central component of our social life and our collective and personal imaginations, and as such can be said to have driven politics and political expectations. My claim here is that the concept's currency has dramatically increased across the social, cultural and political landscape; it has triggered unprecedented interest and allegiance in citizens. The fact that it is a key component of the populist world-view, means that populist politicians are particularly adept at using it. In other words, as authenticity's centrality to political life has grown, so has populism been able to capture the centre-stage of our early twenty-first century politics.

Authenticity rises to prominence as a political concept, but also as a virtue, with the Enlightenment: it emerges as a corollary to the idea of the modern self. A self that is rooted in individual reason and separate from the collective self of the pre-moderns (the family, the tribe, the flock of the faithful). Whereas the latter is mainly defined by its relationships to various hierarchies (family, ruler, God), the modern self emerges as a more autonomous individual (Taylor 1989: 185–207). And that autonomy emanates in part from a new duty to be true to an inner voice. Behaving in a way that embodies that inner voice is the hallmark of authenticity. So, the Enlightenment roots run deep, as do the connections to progress, choice and reason.

Jean Jacques Rousseau, the French eighteenth-century philosopher may be best known to the wider public for his *Social Contract*, but one of his most striking and durable contributions is his *Confessions* – a text that, for critics such as Jean Starobinski (1971), is the first truly modern text, because the protagonist confesses to his inner self's most private desires and most shameful fantasies. These fantasies are not terribly raunchy in the age of *Love Island* and other such reality shows (the volume starts with Rousseau confessing to childhood fantasies about being spanked by the maid with a hairbrush!), but the fact that a prominent political thinker and public intellectual, author of many a draft constitution, should confess to such irredeemably human and imperfect longings is precisely what precipitates, and accounts for, our modern obsession with the concept of authenticity.

Rousseau's confessions are specifically designed to highlight the chasm between ordinary humanity and political society; designed, in other words, to expose the hypocrisy of a ruling class and its institutions (the Church included of course). Rousseau's willingness to reveal so much of his hidden self (as a pledge, a proof of his "good faith") is where it all begins for us: when authenticity starts its journey from the realm of the intimate or private, to the realm of the public and political.[1]

There a number of paradoxes in this story. The first is that authenticity has obviously fuelled the best and worst of our political transformations:

---

1. Rousseau's authenticity could almost be thought of as an early form of what people today might refer to as "virtue-signalling", designed to highlight the chasm between the true self – on which political decisions should be based and societies organized – and appearances.

it has helped us develop a language of human rights, it has enabled us to view difference and diversity as rich expressions of humanity's multiple facets, it has fuelled everything from feminist advances to LGBTQ rights. In other words, it has been firmly on the side of tolerance, understanding, progress and the pluralism that allows diverse societies to function (more) peacefully. But it has also led us to a politics based on Freud's narcissism of small differences, to possible self-righteousness and above all – our concern in this analysis – to a situation in which the new, available means to construct and pursue this authentic persona, seem to have gradually wiped out the belief in both the desirability and the use of representative politics. It reminds me of the 1980s American advert, "This is your brain on drugs" (with an egg sizzling in melted butter); well, "This is your authenticity on social media". If nothing else, populist politics force us to confront this head on because they implicitly hold that any representation is a potential distortion, as opposed to a populist politics that are embodied, direct and immediate.

The darker matter of conspiracy

A second key paradox is that this emphasis on authenticity rooted in democratic politics, the transparency and immediacy driven by digital, and the exploitation of all of them by populism have created a political landscape in which lies and conspiracy theories are rife. Indeed, they are the currency of populist politics. Although paradoxical, this is not a mystery. The demands for transparency and authenticity (especially as they are partially met in the sense that we do have access to more information – both good valid and invalid – about networks, systems, institutions) fuel suspicion.

Far from creating trust, the striving for authenticity through radical transparency creates permanent doubt. No amount of information, and no amount of light can be shed, to completely wipe out the suspicion of dissimulation, and even legitimate and heroic "exposés" now just fuel suspicion. At the moment, the more information we get, the less trusting we are of what it delivers. By exposing everything – including conspiracies, the hidden, the nefarious – our digital era pushes the truth, "the real" further back. It constantly eludes us, either because there are too many rival theories, or because the source can be infinitely questioned. The concept of "deep fakes" encapsulates this perfectly: for now, in the absence of fit-for-purpose institutions, we are faced with a bottomless pit of verification that leads to doubt and, in the absence of absolute certainty and clarity, to conspiracy theories.

This doubt rooted in suspicion is what populism thrives on; its answer is the promise to disrupt, to reveal, to shame those who are accused of dissimulating the truth by promising to be entirely transparent, ordinarily flawed. Not above suspicion, but below it. Just when you think you have hit rock-bottom, populist politics pull another lever and release the trap door to more conspiracy and accusations. The problem, of course, is that in spreading lies and conspiracies, populism is contagious. Those of us who do not start with conspiracy theories, quite quickly alight there. In part because some conspiracies are real – plots do exist and do come to pass – but in part because populist parties leave no choice to their opponents but to defend themselves by pointing to the populist conspiracy to disrupt and sow doubt at all costs. No situation was ever more lose-lose.

A warning, an encouragement and a (light) prophecy

One unavoidable question at this point is where do we go from here? There are several key issues to keep in mind. The first is how we deal with the success of populism's offer.

Relationships, policy and community

Populist parties and leaders promise a different quality of politics, but that promise tends to be "encased" in radically disruptive policy proposals. After all, they have to compete on policy programmes. So, while the disruption and its various tactics are crucial, there is a pretence – or at least an attempt – to make policy promises: to deliver jobs, or housing, or services, to protect life-styles by curtailing migration, etc. The response on behalf of many mainstream parties is often to take the populists at their word and make policy counter-offers that address what are often (although not always) legitimate policy grievances. This, I venture, will lead us nowhere. That is not to say that we shouldn't make policies that help redistribution, that address inequality, that improve people's lives and give them the confidence to live them as they see fit; this is crucial. But it will never be a viable or effective counter-offer to populist politics. For the simple reason that for populist parties, their policy pronouncements are only a means to a relationship with voters, not an end. And so, they will endlessly shift the ground in response to pluralist, mainstream responses: great about the housing policy, but what about the state of schools? OK, so you're addressing schools, but what about wages? You're raising wages? But what about our sense of history? Could you talk-up Christmas? Ah, you're happy to see Christmas celebrated? Well, so says Wilders/Salvini/Marine Le Pen, we'd rather just have all Islamic holidays banned and maybe tax hijabs while we're at it. No? Then you don't care about the real people, etc, etc. The Gilets Jaunes in France are a good illustration of this. While practical concessions were made by President Macron in December 2018 (most significantly, a significant raise in the minimum wage and a scrapping of certain controversial taxes), these did little to dampen protests. What seems to have had more of an impact – although this remains to be seen – in reigning in the populist elements of the Gilets Jaunes, however, is Macron's larger institutional dialogue initiative that has seen him directly interact with both ordinary citizens and their representatives. His own jiu-jitsu move: you say you want to be heard, then let's talk.

Those who argue that populism simply draws attention to the policy failures of representative democracies have a point: failures abound, and people have a right to feel affronted by what is variously, incompetence, difficulty, bad faith, or a combination of all of these. But these same analysts do not seem to have noticed that policy change (of any kind) never seems to satisfy populists. Because the aim of populist politics is to pursue a sense of community through outrage. Shared outrage is the mark of authenticity, and the point is to generate an infinite supply of it.

You could go as far as to say that where mainstream politics pursue a relationship with voters and citizens in order to deliver better policies, populist politics do the very opposite: they gesture towards policy, only in the pursuit of a particular relationship. The point in the latter scenario is to create a community that is more homogenous, more secure, less inclusive and overall, resistant – rather than resilient – to change. The point is the survival of the people, and of the idea of the people. Not the thriving of the multiple, complex, hybrid communities many people live in. Brexit and its attendant debate, is a good illustration of this pursuit of the relationship for its own sake: it is fairly clear at this point, that all of it (whatever shape it ends up taking, including if it remains a never-ending debate) will result in – and has already delivered – diminished economic growth, poorer services and a decrease in general well-being. But the populist answer to that is often: this is a price worth paying, indeed, it is an investment in the kind of political relationships we want to pursue to achieve the resistant community we want.

This is important: no amount of policy delivery will *act as a substitute* for the authentic, direct relationships that parts of the public crave. Policy delivery has to go hand in hand with the authentic relationship. Because the accusation levelled at the mainstream is not that they are not delivering services or policies, but that they are not delivering them because they don't care about, and they don't know, their people.

But what is even more important is that these dynamics should act as clear markers that populism can never be benign. I often come across a reluctance to treat populism as the villain of the piece: sure, they're disruptive. So, what? It forces politicians and policy-makers to face up to their short-comings. Or so the story goes. Yet populism's reliance on disruption, on simplification, on a debased form of authenticity (that is shameless rather than genuine) means that it is inherently corrosive of politics. We can argue that in its devastating impact it forces us to change, but we cannot dismiss that impact as benign. We are being encouraged to view fragmentation, polarization and, sometimes, violence as "authentic" forms of expression. We have seen some of it already: from the murders in Amsterdam, to Italy's record, via the murder of Jo Cox, but also the more anonymous increases in everyday civic violence. We are being encouraged to leave expertise behind and embrace common sense, to deny complexity, to reject diversity and to choose the short-cut of instinct – just as things are possibly more plural, more complex and more delicately balanced than ever before. Populism has ravaged democratic landscapes, leaving the vulnerable (including those who support it) even more vulnerable. It has not allowed a better understanding of people's grievances but rather has manipulated their needs and desires, and offered a distorted reflection, a caricature of what they want, and locked them into a logic of permanent disruption and of ever more disappointment. In this respect populism is not an access to politics, it is a bypassing of it. And its dangers need to be factored in carefully, by looking at the new, deeper dynamics it has unleashed.

So, what would a jiu-jitsu move look like?

What pluralists (as the opposite of populists) need to do is devise their own jiu-jitsu politics. This sort of encouragement is often misunderstood; it is taken to mean that pluralists should reach for populism's so-called "good points" and accommodate them – a politics of concessions: "you may have a point on housing, or on migration, or on globalization. You deserve better." And, of course they do, but this is not jiu-jitsu, this is letting the bully take your lunch money on the grounds that he has a right to lunch too.

The advice here is not to concede, but to use populism's core strength against it, and that means thinking about the new digital landscape in which authenticity has become so central, and so captured by populist politics. This is the obvious arena in which issues of trust, personal efficacy, choice, protection, security will unfold, and are unfolding. These are the new political spaces. Models are emerging – Singapore, Estonia, China, the EU, the US – but none is satisfactory so far. None in fact acknowledges much of an ideological or even an ideational pedigree: each is simply cast as a set of, more or less, state-controlled technocratic frameworks.

Yet data and AI can play a crucially formidable role for pluralists: because they can provide a legitimate terrain for a new form of authenticity to emerge, and a new politics to emerge from that. They can use the power of authenticity unleashed by digital for their own ends; instead of populism's micro-targeting to isolate and manipulate, and its uses of social media to disrupt and divide, pluralists need to construct a form of authentic politics based on using data to understand their citizens more deeply, to micro-target for efficient and tailored delivery. To enable individuals and communities. That means creating and co-creating, designing and co-designing (with tech companies and with communities) institutions – regulations, conventions, legal frameworks, gatherings – that displace populism's crass authenticity by disruption. This would be the jiu-jitsu move to reclaim authenticity by delivering on political relationships based on deep, accurate and fine-grained understanding of citizens and their needs.

The shape of ideologies to come

The argument throughout this book has been that populism has become ever more powerful as a political form because it has exploited a powerful concept that it shares with representative democracy – authenticity. And that it has been able to do so because the digital revolution is making us, as political subjects, much more receptive to populism's promise of authenticity. In this respect, the flourishing of populism has transformed our politics forever.

One of the objections to thinking about populism as an ideology was always that populism – unlike liberalism or communism, and other "isms" – did not have any great foundational texts. This, the argument went, forever relegated it to the ideological minor leagues. But this is to judge ideologies by an outdated yardstick; if anything populism is a demonstration that contemporary ideologies do not need to be rooted in the tradition of great texts. What ideologies will look like remains a mystery, but they may well be rooted in data and information rather than in texts. The new political subject may find her needs for authenticity better met by inspiring algorithms that encapsulate grand ideas about justice, access, voice, equality, rather than, or as well as, by great volumes.

But the most interesting thing about populism is perhaps what it tells us about what ideologies will look like from now on. To return to the astronomy metaphor, it is likely that in the digitalized landscape the dark matter of authenticity will be the main energy driving all ideologies. Authenticity was important to the development of modern democracy; then populism drew its power from the energy that authenticity was lent by the digital revolution; we need to be prepared for the fact that any next emergent or re-emergent ideology will also be shaped (or re-shaped) by both the populist disruption, but also and more fundamentally by the new relevance of authenticity in the imagination and the everyday life of citizens. All issues for the foreseeable will increasingly be viewed through its lens: our connection to each other and to reality is being so fundamentally transformed, that questions of "the real", "the genuine", "the trustworthy" may become even more pressing than questions of justice, of equality, or freedom. Or simply become the inevitable gateway to addressing them. In a word, ideologies ain't what they used to be.

References

Agnew, J. & M. Shin 2016. "Spatializing populism: taking politics to the people of Italy". *Annals of the American Association of Geographers* 107:4, 915–33.

Alfani, G. 2018. "Inequality levels and the perception of inequality over the long run of history". In *Tentacles of Circumstance: The Political Consequences of Inequality*, 13–17. London: Counterpoint.

Anderson, B. 1991. *Imagined Communities: Reflections on the Origin and Spread of Nationalism*. London: Verso.

Arditi, B. 2004. "Populism as a spectre of democracy: a response to Canovan". *Political Studies* 52, 135–43.

Bale, T. 2016. *The Conservative Party from Thatcher to Cameron*, 2nd edition. Cambridge: Polity.

Bale, T. 2018. "Who leads and who follows? The symbiotic relationship between UKIP and the Conservatives – and populism and Euroscepticism". *Politics* 38:3, 263–77.

Barnett, A. 2017. *The Lure of Greatness: England's Brexit and America's Trump*. London: Unbound.

Bartlett, J. *et al.* 2012. "New political actors in Europe: Beppe Grillo and the M5S". Demos Country Briefing Papers. London: Demos.

Bartlett, J. 2017. *Radicals: Outsiders Changing the World*. London: Penguin.

Ben-Ze'ev, A. 2004. *Love Online: Emotions on the Internet*. Cambridge: Cambridge University Press.

Blot, Y. 1992. *Baroque et politique: Le Pen est-il néo-baroque?* Paris: Editions Nationales.

Bobba, G. 2018. "Social media populism: features and 'likeability' of Lega Nord communication on Facebook". *European Political Science*, January, 1–13.

Boichot, L. 2017. "Jean-Luc Mélenchon refuse symboliquement de porter la cravate à l'Assemblée". *Le Figaro*, 27 June. Available at: http://www.lefigaro.fr/politique/2017/06/27/01002-20170627ARTFIG00282-jean-luc-melenchon-refuse-symboliquement-de-porter-la-cravate-a-l-assemblee.php (accessed 20 September 2018).

Bordignon, F. & L. Ceccarini 2013. "Five stars and a cricket: Beppe Grillo shakes Italian politics". *South European Society and Politics* 18:4, 427–49.

Bordignon, F. & L. Ceccarini 2015. "The Five Star Movement: a hybrid actor in the net of state institutions". *Journal of Modern Italian Studies* 20:4, 454–73.

Bot, M. 2017. "Elements of anti-Islam populism: critiquing Geert Wilders' politics of offense with Marcuse and Adorno". *Krisis* 2, 12–25.

Bouvet, L. 2015. *L'Insécurité Culturelle*. Paris: Fayard.

Boyadjian, J. 2015. "Les usages frontistes du web". In *Les Faux-Semblants du Front National: Sociologie d'un parti politique*, 154–60. Paris: Presses de Science Po.

Buruma, I. 2006. *Murder in Amsterdam*. London: Atlantic.

Calise, M. & R. Mannheimer 1982. *Governanti in Italia: un trentennio repubblicano, 1946–1976*. Bologna: Il Mulino.

Canovan, M. 1999. "Trust the people! Populism and the two-faces of democracy". *Political Studies* 47, 2–16.

Coe, J. 2018. *Middle England*. London: Penguin.

Counterpoint 2011–. "The threats of populism: Europe's reluctant radicals". Available at: http://counterpoint.uk.com/ideaslab/reluctant-radicals-2/ (accessed 22 March 2019).

Counterpoint 2017. *Tentacles of Circumstance: The Political Consequences of Inequality*. London: Counterpoint. Available at: http://counterpoint.uk.com/a-new-bridges-pamphlet-is-coming-out-the-tentacles-of-circumstance-the-political-consequences-of-inequality/ (accessed 22 March 2019).

Dalton, R. & M. Kuechler 1990. *Challenging the Political Order*. New York: Oxford University Press.

Dalton, R. 2007. *Democratic Challenges, Democratic Choices: The Erosion of Political Support in Advanced Industrial Democracies*. New York: Oxford University Press.

Dézé, A. 2015. *Le 'nouveau' Front National en question*. Paris: Fondation Jean Jaurès.

Dorling, D. & S. Tomlinson 2019. *Rule Britannia: Brexit and the End of Empire*. London: Biteback.

Eatwell, R. & M. Goodwin 2018. *National Populism: The Revolt Against Liberal Democracy*. Abingdon: Routledge.

Einar Thorsen, D. & A. Lie (DATE), *What is Neoliberalism?* University of Oslo. Available at: http://folk.uio.no/daget/neoliberalism.pdf (accessed 22 March 2019).

Enli, G. 2016. "Trust me, I'm authentic". In A. Bruns *et al.* (eds) *The Routledge Companion to Social Media and Politics*, {pages}. Abingdon: Routledge.

Eribon, D. 2009. *Retour á Rheims: Une Théorie du Sujet*. Paris: Artheme Fayard.

Escalona, F. & M. Vieira 2014. "Le sens et le rôle de la résistance à l'UE pour le Parti de gauche". *Politique Européenne* 43:1, 68–92.

Evans, G. & A. Menon 2017. *Brexit and British Politics*. Cambridge: Polity.

Fernandez, G. 2018. "Marion Maréchal (Le Pen): queremos gestar algo como un gobierno en sombra". *El Confidencial*, 23 September. Available at: https://www.elconfidencial.com/mundo/2018-09-23/entrevista-marion-merechal-escuela-pensamiento-lyon_1619185/ (accessed 15 September 2018).

Fieschi, C. 2004a. *In the Shadow of Democracy: Fascism, Populism and the French Fifth Republic*. Manchester: Manchester University Press.

Fieschi, C. 2004b. Introduction to special issue on "Populism". *Journal of Political Ideologies*, 89:3, 235–40.

Fieschi, C. 2005. "Far right alarmism". *Prospect Magazine*, 17 March. Available at: https://www.prospectmagazine.co.uk/magazine/farrightalarmism (accessed 22 March 2019).

Fieschi, C. 2013. "Introduction". In *Populist Fantasies: European Revolts in Context*. London: Counterpoint.

Fieschi, C. 2017. "Protecting the Grey Zones". *New Associations: British Psychoanalytic Council* 24, Winter 2017.

Fieschi, C. (n.d.). "Welcome to the new Colosseum". Available at: http://counterpoint.uk.com/welcome-to-the-new-coliseum-abdication-surrender-and-the-referendum-moment-in-european-politics/ (accessed 22 March 2019).

Fieschi, C. & P. Heywood 2004. "Trust, cynicism and populist anti-politics". *Journal of Political Ideologies* 89:3, 289–309.

Fieschi, C., M. Morris & L. Caballero-Sosa 2012. *Recapturing the Reluctant Radical.* London: Counterpoint.

Frank, T. 2004. *What's the Matter with Kansas? How Conservatives won the Heart of America.* New York: Henry Holt.

Freeden, F. 1998. *Ideologies and Political Theory: A Conceptual Approach.* Oxford: Oxford University Press.

Georgiadou, V., L. Rori & C. Roumanias 2018. "Mapping the European far right in the 21st century: a meso-level analysis". *Electoral Studies* 54, 103–15.

Gombin, J. 2016. *Le Front National: Va-t-elle diviser la France?* Paris: Eyrolles.

Goodhart, D. 2017. *The Road to Somewhere: The Populist Revolt and the Future of Politics.* London: Hurst.

Griffin, R. 1993. *The Nature of Fascism.* London: Routledge.

Hahl, O., M. Kim & E. Zukerman Sivan 2018. "The authentic appeal of the lying demagogue: proclaiming the deeper truth about political illegitimacy". *American Sociological Review* 83:1, 1–33.

Hamburger, J. 2018. "Whose populism? The mixed messages of la France Insoumise". *Dissent* 65:3, 101–10.

Harmon-Jones, E. & P. Winkeman 2007. *Social Neuroscience.* New York: Guilford.

Harvey, D. 2010. *A Brief History of Neoliberalism.* Oxford: Oxford University Press.

Hay, C. 1995. "Rethinking crisis: narratives of the new right and constructions of crisis". *Rethinking Marxism: A Journal of Economics, Culture and Society* 8:2, 60–76.

Hirsi Ali, A. & G. Wilders 2003. "Het is tijd voor een liberale jihad" [It is Time for a Liberal Jihad]. NRC Handelsblad.

Hoschild, A. 2016. *Strangers in their Own Land: Anger and Mourning in the American Right.* New York: New Press.

House of Commons Treasury Committee 2016. "The economic and financial costs and benefits of the UK's EU membership". Available at: https://publications.parliament. uk/pa/cm201617/cmselect/cmtreasy/122/122.pdf (accessed 22 March 2019).

Howarth, D., A. Norval & Y. Stavrakakis (eds) 2005. *Discourse Theory and Political Analysis.* Manchester: Manchester University Press.

Inglehart, R. 1990. *Culture Shift.* Princeton, NJ: Princeton University Press.

Inglehart, R. & P. Norris 2018. *Cultural Backlash: Trump, Brexit and the Rise of Authoritarian Populism.* Cambridge: Cambridge University Press.

Kain, P J. 1990. "Rousseau, the general will and individual liberty". *History of Philosophy Quarterly* 7:3, 315-334.

Kahneman, D. 2011. *Thinking, Fast and Slow.* New York: Farrar, Strauss & Giroux.

King's College Policy Institute 2018. "Public wrong on key facts around Brexit and impact of EU membership, new study finds". *Brexit Misperceptions,* 28 October. Available at: https://www.kcl.ac.uk/sspp/policy-institute/news/newsrecords/2018/public-wrong-on-key-facts-around-brexit-and-impact-of-eu-membership-new-study-finds.aspx (accessed 22 March 2019).

Kirsch, A. 2008. "Obama Bests Clinton At Craft of Writing', *The New York Sun,* 3 March.

Klingemann, H.-D. 1999. "Political support in the 1990s". In P. Norris (ed.) *Critical Citizens: Global Support for Democratic Government,* 1–27. Oxford: Oxford University Press.

Klingemann, H.-D. & D. Fuchs (eds) 1995. *Citizens and the State*. Oxford: Oxford University Press.

Lange de, S. 2007. "A new winning formula? The programmatic appeal of the radical right". *Party Politics* 13:4, 411–35.

Levy, D., B. Aslan & D. Bironzo 2016. "The press and the referendum campaign". In D. Jackson, E. Thorsen & D. Wring (eds), *EU Referendum Analysis 2016: Media, Voters and the Campaign, Early Reflections from Leading UK Academics*. Centre for the Study of Journalism, Culture and Community, Bournemouth University.

MacWilliams, M. 2016. *The Rise of Trump: America's Authoritarian Spring*. Amherst, MA: Amherst College Press.

Mailland, J. 2017. "Minitel, the open network before the internet". *The Atlantic*, 16 June.

Marchlewska, M. *et al.* 2018. "Populism as identity politics: perceived in-group disadvantage, collective narcissism, and support for populism". *Social Psychological and Personality Science* 9:2, 151–62.

Marcus, G. 2002. *The Sentimental Citizen: Emotion in Democratic Politics*. University Park, PA: Penn State University Press.

Mazzoleni, G. & R. Bracciale 2018. "Socially mediated populism: the communication strategies of political leaders on Facebook". *Palgrave Communications* 50:4, 1–10.

McAuley, J. 2018. "A scion of France's Le Pen family opens a training academy for a new far-right elite". *The Washington Post*, 14 September. Available at: https://www.washingtonpost.com/world/europe/a-scion-of-frances-le-pen-family-opens-a-training-academy-for-a-new-far-right-elite/2018/09/14/f3121292-b04c-11e8-8b53-50116768e499_story.html?utm_term=.11f8174525d9 (accessed 19 September 2018).

Mestre, A. & C. Monot 2015. "Les réseaux du Front National". In *Les Faux-Semblants du Front National: Sociologie d'un parti politique*, 51–76. Paris: Presses de Science Po.

Moffitt, B. 2015. "How to perform crisis: a model for understanding the key role of crisis in contemporary populism". *Government and Opposition* 50:2, pages?

Moffitt, B. 2016. *The Global Rise of Populism: Performance, Political Style and Representation*. Stanford, CA: Stanford University Press.

Moffitt, B. & S. Tormey 2014. "Rethinking populism: politics, mediatisation and political style". *Political Studies* 62:2, 381–97.

Morris, M. & P. Kreko 2014. "The conspiratorial mindset in Europe". OpenDemocracy, 29 January. Available at: https://www.opendemocracy.net/can-europe-make-it/marley-morris-p%C3%A9ter-krek%C3%B3/conspiratorial-mindset-in-europe (accessed 19 March 2019).

Mudde, C. 2007. *Populist Radical Right Parties in Europe*. Cambridge: Cambridge University Press.

Mudde, C. & C. Rovira Kaltwasser (eds) 2013. *Populism in Europe and the Americas: Threat or Corrective for Democracy?* Cambridge: Cambridge University Press.

Mullen, A. 2016. "Leave vs Remain: the digital battle". In D. Jackson, E. Thorsen & D. Wring (eds) *EU Referendum Analysis 2016: Media, Voters and the Campaign, Early Reflections from Leading UK Academics*. Centre for the Study of Journalism, Culture and Community, Bournemouth University.

Muller, J.-W. 2017. *What is Populism?* London: Penguin.

Newell, J. 2010. *The Politics of Italy*. Cambridge: Cambridge University Press.

Offe, C. 1999. "How can we trust our fellow citizens?" In M. Warren (ed.) *Democracy and Trust*, 42–87. Cambridge: Cambridge University Press.

Offer, A. 2006. *The Challenge of Affluence: Self-Control and Well-being in the United States and Britain since 1950*. Oxford: Oxford University Press.

Oliver, J. & W. Rahn 2016. "Rise of the *Trumpenvolk*: populism in the 2016 election". *Annals of the American Academy of Political and Social Science* 667:1, 189–206.

Panizza, F. (ed.) 2005. *Populism and the Mirror of Democracy*. London: Verso.

Phillips, A. 2012. *Missing Out: In Praise of the Unlived Life*. London: Penguin.

Renwick, A., M. Flinders & W. Jennings 2016. "Calming the storm, fighting falsehoods, fig-leaves and fairy tales". In D. Jackson, E. Thorsen & D. Wring (eds) *EU Referendum Analysis 2016: Media, Voters and the Campaign, Early Reflections from Leading UK Academics*. Centre for the Study of Journalism, Culture and Community, Bournemouth University.

Riotta, G. 2013. "Seasons of Italian populism". In *Populist Fantasies: European Revolts in Context*, 571–609. London: Counterpoint.

Rousseau, J. J. 1978. *On the Social Contract*. New York: St Martin's Press.

Rushkoff, D. 2016. "The new nationalism of Brexit and Trump is the product of the digital age". *Fastcoexist*, 7 July.

Sandbu, M. 2018. "Is culture or economics at the root of our strange politics?" In *Tentacles of Circumstance: The Political Consequences of Inequality*, 32–8. London: Counterpoint.

Starobinski, J. 1971. *Jean-Jacques Rousseau, la Transparence et l'obstacle*. Paris: Gallimard.

Stavrakakis, Y. 2000. "On the emergence of Green ideology: the dislocation factor in Green politics". In D. Howarth, A. Norval & Y. Stavrakakis (eds) *Discourse Theory and Political Analysis*. Manchester: Manchester University Press.

Stavrakakis, Y. & A. Jager 2018. "Accomplishments and limitations of the 'new' mainstream in contemporary populism studies". *European Journal of Social Theory* 21:4, 547–65.

Stille, A. 2010. *Citizen Berlusconi. Il Cavalier Miracolo. La vita, le imprese, la politica*. Milan: Garzanti Libri.

Stille, A. 2018. "How Matteo Salvini pulled Italy to the far right", *The Guardian*, 9 August. Available at: https://www.theguardian.com/news/2018/aug/09/how-matteo-salvini-pulled-italy-to-the-far-right (accessed 22 March 2019).

Stothard, M. 2017. "National Front rock star keeps French hardliners in thrall". *Financial Times*, 31 March. Available at: https://www.ft.com/content/a865e5fc-145d-11e7-80f4-13e067d5072c (accessed 20 September 2018).

Taggart, P. 2000. *Populism*. Buckingham: Open University Press.

Taguieff, P.-A. 2005. *La Foire aux illuminés: Esoterisme, théorie du complot, extrémisme*. Paris: Mille et une nuits.

Tarchi, M. 2008. "Italy: a country of many populisms". In D. Albertazzi & D. McDonnell (eds) *Twenty-First Century Populism: The Spectre of Western European Democracy*, {pages}. Basingstoke: Palgrave Macmillan.

Tarchi, M. 2015. "Italy: the promised land of populism?" *Contemporary Italian Politics* 7:3, 273–85.

Taylor, C. 1989. *Sources of the Self: The Making of the Modern Identity*. Cambridge, MA: Harvard University Press.

Temin, P. 2017. *The Vanishing Middle Class: Prejudice and Power in a Dual Economy*. Cambridge, MA: MIT Press.

Thompson, E. P. 1971. "The moral economy of the English crowd in the eighteenth century". *Past & Present* 50, 76–136.

Tremblay, P. 2017. "La moquerie et l'insulte chez Mélenchon? 'Parfois faut dire à un patron que c'est un con'". *Huffington Post*, 25 May. Available at: https://www.huffingtonpost.fr/2017/05/25/la-moquerie-et-linsulte-chez-melenchon-parfois-faut-dire-a-un_a_22109084/ (accessed 19 September 2018).

Trilling, L. 1971. *Sincerity and Authenticity*. Cambridge, MA: Harvard University Press.

Tronconi, F. 2018. "The Italian Five Star movement during the crisis: towards normalisation?" *South European Society and Politics* 23:1, 163–80.

Turkle, S. 1984. *The Second Self: Computers and the Human Spirit*. Cambridge, MA: MIT Press.

Turkle, S. 2011. *Alone Together: Why We Expect More from Technology and Less from Each Other*. New York: Basic Books.

Umbach, M. & M. Humphrey 2017. *Authenticity: The Cultural History of a Political Concept*. London: Palgrave Macmillan.

Vance, J. 2016. *Hillbilly Elegy: A Memoir of a Family and Culture in Crisis*. New York: Harper.

Wagner, M. 2014. "Fear and anger in Great Britain: blame assignment and emotional reactions to the financial crisis". *Political Behavior* 36:3, 683–703.

Westen, D. 2007. *The Political Brain: The Role of Emotion in Deciding the Fate of the Nation*. New York: Public Affairs.

Žižek, S. 2004. "What Rumsfeld doesn't know that he knows about Abu Ghraib". *In These Times*, 21 May. Available at: http://inthesetimes.com/article/747/what_rumsfeld_doesn_know_that_he_knows_about_abu_ghraib (accessed 22 March 2019).

Index

Note: numbers in brackets preceded by *n* refer to footnotes.